THE CHURCH & THE AMERICAN TEENAGER

ZONDERVAN/YOUTH SPECIALTIES BOOKS

Professional Resources
Advanced Peer Counseling in Youth Groups
Called to Care
Developing Student Leaders
Feeding Your Forgotten Soul
Great Fundraising Ideas for Youth Groups
Help! I'm a Volunteer Youth Worker!
High School Ministry
How to Recruit and Train Volunteer
  Youth Workers (*previously released*
  as Unsung Heroes)
Junior High Ministry (Revised Edition)
The Ministry of Nurture
Organizing Your Youth Ministry
Peer Counseling in Youth Groups
Road Trip
The Youth Minister's Survival Guide
Youth Ministry Nuts and Bolts
The Youth Workers Promo Kit

Discussion Starter Resources
Amazing Tension Getters
Get 'Em Talking
High School TalkSheets
Hot Talks
Junior High TalkSheets
More High School TalkSheets
More Junior High TalkSheets
Option Plays
Parent Ministry TalkSheets
Teach 'Toons
Tension Getters
Tension Getters Two

Special Needs and Issues
The Complete Student Missions Handbook
Divorce Recovery for Teenagers
Ideas for Social Action
Intensive Care: Helping Teenagers in Crisis
Rock Talk
Teaching the Truth About Sex
Up Close and Personal: How to Build
  Community in Your Youth Group

Youth Ministry Programming
Adventure Games
Creative Programming Ideas
  for Junior High Ministry
Creative Socials and Special Events
Good Clean Fun
Good Clean Fun, Volume 2
Great Games for City Kids

Great Ideas for Small Youth Groups
Greatest Skits on Earth
Greatest Skits on Earth, Volume 2
Holiday Ideas for Youth Groups
  (Revised Edition)
Junior High Game Nights
More Junior High Game Nights
On-Site: 40 On-Location Youth Programs
Play It! Great Games for Groups
Play It Again! More Great Games
  for Groups
Super Sketches for Youth Ministry
Teaching the Bible Creatively
The Youth Specialties Handbook
  for Great Camps and Retreats

4th-6th Grade Ministry
Attention Grabbers for 4th-6th Graders
4th-6th Grade TalkSheets
Great Games for 4th-6th Graders
How to Survive Middle School
Incredible Stories
More Attention Grabbers for 4th-6th Graders
More Great Games for 4th-6th Graders
More Quick and Easy Activities
  for 4th-6th Graders
Quick and Easy Activities for 4th-6th Graders
Teach 'Toons

Clip Art
ArtSource™ Volume 1—Fantastic Activities
ArtSource™ Volume 2—Borders, Symbols,
  Holidays, and Attention Getters
ArtSource™ Volume 3—Sports
ArtSource™ Volume 4—Phrases and Verses
ArtSource™ Volume 5—Amazing Oddities
  and Appalling Images
ArtSource™ Volume 6—Spiritual Topics
Youth Specialties Clip Art Book
Youth Specialties Clip Art Book, Volume 2

Video
Next Time I Fall In Love Video Curriculum
Understanding Your Teenager
  Video Curriculum
Video Spots for Junior High Game Nights

Student Books
Going the Distance
Grow for It Journal
Next Time I Fall in Love
Next Time I Fall in Love Journal

THE CHURCH & THE AMERICAN TEENAGER

TONY CAMPOLO

Formerly titled *Growing Up in America*

WHAT WORKS AND WHAT DOESN'T WORK IN YOUTH MINISTRY

ZondervanPublishingHouse
Grand Rapids, Michigan

A Division of HarperCollinsPublishers

To my son,
Bart Anthony Campolo,
who makes me proud

Contents

Introduction

WHAT IS A SOCIOLOGY OF YOUTH MINISTRY?

Sociology is a study of what people create when they interact with each other. Those who practice this "science" try to come up with theories that explain how societies give birth to values, beliefs, and patterns of expected behavior. We all know that these creations of society—these values, beliefs, and patterns of behavior—in turn re-create their creators. To put it another way, sociology is the study of how people create societies and cultures and how they, in turn, are controlled by what they create.

Over the years, sociologists' findings have been useful to those whose vocations involve working with people. Social workers have applied sociological principles with their clients. Family counselors have valued sociological insights about how cultural factors influence sexual behavior and family patterns. Managers of businesses and industries have used sociological findings to create good labor relations and efficient production.

This book will explore how sociological findings help youth workers. First, sociological theories and discoveries can help explain why teenagers are the way they are and what methods can be used to help them become the kinds of persons Christians ought to be. Second, sociological insights can help youth workers to understand more fully their own role in the ecclesiastical systems that employ them and that cause them many stresses and strains. Third, sociology can help youth workers to understand not only the world in which we live and work but also how to deal with that world as it impacts all that we are and do.

This book is in no way comprehensive in handling such topics. Rather, it stands on its own as the attempt of one sociologist, who is himself involved in youth ministry, to apply the findings of his so-called "value-free" discipline to the very value-laden role of the Christian youth worker.

WHY THEOLOGY FROM A SOCIOLOGICAL PERSPECTIVE?

Some of what you'll read in this book may seem a bit off-beat, a radical departure from more traditional approaches to religion. That's because theology usually has been written in philosophical terms, in response to questions posed by philosophy. Consequently, my attempt to use sociological language and to respond to sociological questions may come across as a bit strange. Instead of dealing with Plato, Aristotle, Kant, and Hegel in putting together a theology, I've focused on the concerns of sociologists like Durkheim, Marx, Weber, and Goffman.

I'm convinced that a sociological theology is the coming thing. This belief stems first of all from the fact that in the post-Hegelian era, philosophy has almost died. It's not that the concerns of our time don't require philosophical analy-sis—they do. The trouble is that philosophy provides little help for such tasks. A survey of what is going on at modern secular universities provides ample evidence of this sudden demise. All that seems to be left of it are a few courses in existentialism and a handful of others in logical positivism. Existentialism is more an anti-rational rebellion against logical positivism than a thoughtful solution to our everyday problems. Logical positivism really says nothing and only ends up trying to say nothing with empirical precision.

Sociology has stepped into the void and is the discipline that presently is defining the issues with which theology must grapple. Concerns about economic and political justice, which have become major issues for modern theologians, emerge more out of sociological analysis than out of philosophical reflection.

Sociologists, rather than philosophers, provide the *best* insights on problems like alienation, anomie, and the loss of community. Even those who are trying to understand what makes *homo sapiens* human will probably find more help from the social sciences than from contemporary philosophers who study linguistic analysis or who probe the absurdity of the human condition. As a matter of fact, sociology instead of philosophy is probably the best undergraduate preparation for those who are going to seminary and into ministry.

Perhaps the time is ripe for a new discipline that brings together sociology and theology. A scholar in one of our Christian colleges has even given it a name—sociotheology. If such a discipline does develop, I would hope this book provides some contributions to it. And in any event, I hope that what I've written will help youth workers do their job a little better. It's to this end that I ask you to do theology from a sociological perspective.

WHAT'S IN THIS BOOK

This book is divided into three parts. Part 1 explains how society conditions teenagers' behavior and how youth workers can help them to be Christians in the face of cultural influences that work against the Christian lifestyle.

Part 2 is very practical; it provides a sociological perspective on how youth workers can reach their peak effectiveness with teenagers in such areas of their jobs as counseling and programing meetings. It explores the socio-logical implications of issues such as the shape of the American family, the influence of TV and affluence on young people, the role of crisis counseling in shaping a young person's theology, and the effect of mass meetings on young people.

Part 3 is designed to help youth workers in self-examination. Because they practice youth ministry within the institutional church, youth workers find themselves subject to both role conflicts and peculiar seductive situations that can leave them spiritually and psychologically dissipated. I have tried to analyze these stresses and strains and to provide some guidance to youth workers struggling with such questions as: Why do so many youth workers leave the youth ministry? How can I handle power struggles between staff members? How do I work in an affluent church without becoming seduced by affluence? How can I maintain spiritual vitality for myself and my youth group? What are the advantages and disadvantages of professionalizing youth work?

Much of the material in the last two sections of this book is based upon articles I've written for *Youthworker*, a journal published by Youth Specialties. The people of Youth Specialties have given their permission to reproduce this material that has been so much a part of my effort to develop a sociology of youth ministry, and I'm grateful for their cooperation. I send special thanks to Noel Becchetti, Tic Long, Wayne Rice, Mike Yaconelli, and all those who make Youth Specialties such a lively and creative organization.

PART 1

THE MAKING OF THE AMERICAN TEENAGER

1 What's the World Doing to Kids, Anyway?

Wherever I go, I'm asked the same question: "What are young people like these days?"

It seems to me that those who ask that question are asking me to sum up all the relevant sociological discoveries about young people in a profound sentence or two. I respond by explaining that sociology isn't a very exact science and that, at best, I can offer a few dubious opinions derived from my limited observations and deduced from some generally accepted theoretical perspectives. All of this simply says that what follows is but one man's opinion about why young people are the way they are.

Young people are influenced by the dominant values of our culture. Three of the most pervasive values are success, consumerism, and personal happiness.

SUCCESS COMPETITIVELY ACHIEVED

It takes no brilliance to discern that few of society's values loom as important in shaping the lives and psyches of our young people as success gained through competition. Will Herberg, in his book *Protestant, Catholic, Jew,* argues that this particular cultural value functions very much as a religious imperative among American young people.[1] "Success competitively achieved" is an unspoken proposition of the belief system of all Americans. To succeed seems to be a God-ordained obligation; to fail, for most Americans, is an unforgivable sin.

But there's more to it than that. In America, young people are not only driven to succeed but also compelled to measure their success in terms of the accomplishments of others. It isn't enough to do your best. You must do *better than your peers* if your accomplishments are to provide a sense of fulfillment.

As a college professor, I'm always reminded of this reality when I hand back test papers. Students are every bit as interested in the grades of their friends as they are in their own. I've seen students thrilled with *C*s on their exams as long as everybody else in their class did worse. This is because, in America, it isn't enough for the individual to succeed. It's also necessary for his or her peers to fail. Our culture bombards our young people with the goal to be "number one." To be "the best" is part of the psyche of American young people.

This drive to achieve competitive success makes it difficult for young people to develop loving relationships. If they're brought up to believe that they must be better than others, intimacy becomes difficult to establish. Every romantic relationship teenagers experience ends up being a contest that has a winner and a loser. Dating patterns are affected: Girls learn early that the only way to hold on to a boyfriend is to be careful not to threaten his unspoken claims to superiority. Girls learn to downplay their skills in tennis games and their accomplishments in school work because they realize that only boys who feel superior to girls can feel comfortable with them.

Competition is drilled into the consciousness of American young people from the earliest stages of their socialization. It isn't only the overt message that they pick up at home and school; it's the covert message that is subtly communicated through educational methods. I recall with some degree of pain a childhood experience that gives blatant evidence of what I'm talking about here.

I arrived at school with my best friend, Harry. I liked

going to school with Harry. He was the smartest kid in our fifth-grade class, and I was proud to be his good buddy. On this day we had no sooner arrived in school and taken our places than the teacher announced what at first seemed to be good news. She said that we were not going to start with our regular school work; instead, we were going to play a game of baseball. I was overjoyed because I was the best one in the class in baseball. But then she broke the bad news. We were going to play *spelling* baseball. I was crushed. Spelling was my worst subject. As the son of Italian immigrants, I never did well in spelling. (This isn't because Italians are stupid but because the English language is absurd.) It was hard for me to figure out such things as why the first letter of the word *pneumonia* should be a *p.*

The teacher chose two captains, and the captains, in turn, were to select their team members. Harry was chosen captain because he was the best speller in the class. The other captain was a girl named Mary. Mary was one of those girls who made kids like me sick. She was just too cute for words and too perfect in everything she did. She wore cute little ruffled dresses and had prissy mannerisms that disgusted me.

As the captains began to take turns choosing the members of their teams, I figured for sure Harry would choose me. After all, I was his best friend. But Harry looked right past me. It was almost as if I were not in the room. He picked some of the other people right around me. I waved my hand furiously in his face, but my hand may as well have been invisible. He went on picking other people, and so did Mary. And neither of them wanted me.

The teacher was convinced that she was teaching us spelling, but I was learning another lesson that day. I was learning that friendship really isn't very important, at least not as far as this game was concerned. The only thing that mattered to Harry was whether or not I could spell competitively. If I had been a successful speller, Harry would have wanted me. But because I wasn't, he ignored me, despite the fact that we were supposed to be buddies.

The two of them went on picking people until there were only two of us left in the class. Even when the selection was down to two, Harry didn't want me. Finally the teacher assigned me to his team.

On the first round of the game, I blew it on the word *grasshopper.*I didn't know it had two *p*'s. The teacher matter-of-factly announced that I had struck out and should take my seat. At that moment I didn't think anyone could be lonelier than I felt as the first one out in the spelling baseball game. With drooping shoulders and sunken chest, I made my way to my seat. The people on the other team cheered my failure while those on my own team booed me. My humiliation was complete.

The teacher then turned to the other team and asked, "Does anyone *here* know how to spell *grasshopper?*"

Little Mary knew. She answered with flair. "Grass-hopper," she said. "G-R-A-S-S-H-O-P-P-E-R." With each letter, she swung her shoulders proudly. And with each letter, I felt the pain of a knife being pushed into my stomach.

If lesson number one was that friendship isn't as important as success, the second lesson of the morning was that Mary's success was constructed on my failure. Her glory was dependent upon my humiliation. I survived that elementary-school experience, but I didn't do so unscathed.

The competitive lifestyle engendered by American society creates tremendous fear and self-doubt in the psyche of young people. They feel that to survive they must compete with everyone else; yet, on the other hand, they live in fear of failure. They don't feel as if they're worth much unless they win in the many competitive options that confront them from the time they play Little League baseball or sell cookies for their Brownie troop to the time they take their SATs. For many adolescents, competition takes the joy out of most of what they do during their high-school days.

Graduation day is greeted with mixed emotions because it's perceived as a public declaration of failure by some even as it serves as a public declaration of achievement for others. For most graduates, this day serves as a reminder that they've failed to achieve anything but mediocrity. Most people don't get those special prizes given to "the best" in French, Spanish, and algebra. Most don't get to be valedictorians or salutatorians. They simply must pretend to applaud benevolently while "the elect," who always seem to be the winners, get the public adulation that they themselves crave. What makes graduation day particularly hard for "average" teenagers is that they have to invite their parents to join them in applauding the special kids. Their parents tell them it doesn't matter that they won no glory or prizes, but the "average" kids know that their parents had hoped for better. It's no wonder that so many of them go out and get drunk when the graduation ceremonies are over.

POPULARITY AND PEER PRESSURE

I don't want to convey the idea that sports and academics are the only arenas of competition for American teenagers. One measurement of social success is even more important to them—the all-important index of high-school success: *popularity*. Whatever else is achieved, everyone knows that being "popular" is the ultimate prize for the American teenager. Without popularity, academic achievers are labeled "bookworms," and star athletes are labeled "jocks." You may rightly ask, "What does it profit a teenager if he or she gains the whole world but loses popularity?" When all is said and done, parents gain their greatest satisfaction when their kids are among the most popular. How parents love to say, "The phone never stops ringing."

According to some of America's most insightful sociologists, popularity is easily measured by how well one does with the opposite sex.[2] In the end, one's popularity is often determined by how many girls like you if you're a guy, and how many guys like you if you're a girl. Even members of the teenagers' own sex evaluate him or her by how well he or she does with members of the opposite sex. Parents know that their daughter is a success if boys have to be swept off the front porch or that their son is a success if the girls are calling *him* on the telephone.

Parents don't make it easy on teenagers who have to compete for a favorable position on the popularity ladder. On the one hand, they make it abundantly clear to their children how important it is to be popular. On the other hand, they're always harping on their kids not to go along with the crowd. Parents give endless lectures on how they expect their children to be faithful to what they know is right even when "the gang" is doing the opposite. Consequently, kids are caught in a dilemma: "Should I do what is right and risk losing popularity, or should I be as popular as my parents want me to be even if I have to compromise many of the things I know are right?"

Studies among teenagers reveal that the primary factor inducing them to use drugs is the desire to be popular with a peer group that is into drugs. We seem to have the idea that teenagers get into drugs because some "pusher" hanging around school yards seduces them. In reality, most kids get into drugs because their peers think it's "cool," and they'll go looking for a pusher if one isn't conveniently hanging around. Young people know drugs are wrong, but being "in" with the gang is often more important to them than doing what they know is right.

Sex researchers have long known that teenagers often compromise their moral standards because not to do so would put their popularity at risk. Furthermore, it's a sad fact that many unpopular girls learn that boys begin to hang around them and call them on the telephone when they "loosen up a bit." It's hard to guess how many of them have devalued themselves for no other reason than to escape the anonymity that usually is ascribed to "ordinary girls."

THE FRUIT OF COMPETITION: APATHY AND HOSTILITY

When faced with the social system's awesome demands to achieve—be it for grades, for trophies in sports, or for popularity—many young people choose simply not to compete. Fearing failure, they find that the easiest route is often simply to give up and declare that they don't care.

In the face of what seems to be apathy, many parents will run to school counselors and have long meetings with church youth workers, insisting that their son or daughter would achieve great things if he or she would just apply himself or herself. Parents will pay psychotherapists huge sums of money for some clues to their children's lack of motivation. In all of their scrambling for answers, these parents often ignore an obvious fact—that their children may not be motivated to try because they're dreadfully afraid they'll fail. Many teenagers prefer to believe that they *could* have succeeded if they'd tried, rather than to try—and find out. After all, to try is to risk failing.

Fear of failure breeds apathy in teenagers, and the displeasure of their parents over their apathy only serves to make them hostile. This hostility is seen in many aspects of the youth subculture. I became very aware of this one evening when, being too tired to watch anything else on television, I turned to the MTV channel and watched a few of the rock-music videos that are popular with many teenagers. I was shocked and dismayed by what I saw. I expected that the MTV videos would be sexually suggestive, and they were. I knew that the dress styles and makeup of the singers would look decadent, and they did. But what surprised me was the hostility of the musicians—the hate in their faces, the explosions of anger in their wild stage antics.

At first glance, these rock stars had appeared to be

merely entertainers; yet, as I watched, I realized that they articulated the hostility of a generation of kids who have been made to feel like losers in a society that demands they play competitive games. These singers were giving a lot of hurting kids the opportunity vicariously to "give the finger" to parents, teachers, and preachers. These wild people armed with guitars were telling the referees of society's games to get off their backs.

Suddenly, it no longer seemed strange to me that rock musicians are the idols of so many disaffected kids. Apparently, these video stars have the ability to give expression to a lot of groanings that cannot be uttered. The singing Madonna and her kin are telling an oppressive establishment to leave the kids alone. The medium is their message, and their message is "to hell with what you expect us to be."

I conclude that the stars of the videos are defiers of the establishment. It isn't at all surprising that teenagers love them and that the custodians of the established order of things consider them dangerous.

CHRISTIAN FELLOWSHIP AS THE BALM OF GILEAD

How can we as Christians counteract this competitive spirit and all the damage it does? How can youth workers help young people move beyond society's standard of success? **Eliminate competition in your youth group.** Caring youth workers will want to restructure their ministries and programs to provide some deliverance for teenagers who are stressed out by living in a highly competitive social system. They will seek to provide an environment in which acceptance doesn't have to be earned, in which young people will feel loved without having to prove themselves, and in which the measurements of success so important in high schools—sports, grades, and popularity—will be ignored.

How can youth workers achieve these goals? They can make sure that their programs don't encourage domination by super stars. Sports activities may seem like a healthy outlet for youth groups, but they are unhealthy if they simply become opportunities for the glorification of the already glorified or the degradation of the already put down. Sensitive youth workers will encourage activities that neutralize the superior skills of some of the participants and that make having fun as a group the main purpose of recreation.

I know of one youth worker who set up a volleyball game in which the net was fifteen feet high. Her youth-group members played with a weather balloon instead of a volleyball, and the game was a crazy delight. Everyone participated as equals. The super jocks quickly learned that they couldn't dominate and that the fun came from cheering the movement of a balloon more influenced by the wind than by their athletic prowess. Those who were not jocks quickly gained confidence as full-fledged participants in the game. The game had everybody laughing, and winning was no big thing.

It's also unwise for church youth groups to sponsor activities that favor those who are good looking. As far as I'm concerned, dances fall into this category. I question the rightness of Christian youth groups having dances—not because dances "stimulate the lusts of the flesh" as some Puritan critics might suggest, but rather because dances threaten those who don't feel good about their physical appearance. Any program or activity that necessitates being favored by members of the opposite sex is likely to be avoided by those who don't think of themselves as glamorous or handsome.

Given a choice between holding a dance or sponsoring a "walk" for some worthy cause, like raising money to feed the hungry, sensitive youth workers should commit themselves to the latter project. Participation in a dance requires a teenager to obtain a partner of the opposite sex. On the other hand, a walk for a worthy cause includes anyone who wants to help the poor. With the walk, teenagers who are uncertain about how they are coming across to members of the opposite sex do not risk rejection. And there's no competition, pressure to succeed, or possibility that a person can lose.

Minister to the "average" kid. It's tempting for youth workers to pay special attention to extreme "winners" or extreme "losers." The winners (sports stars, class presidents, and members of the National Honor Society) can easily be seen as instruments for building attendance at youth meetings. It's tempting for youth workers to *use* them to "sell" youth programs.

It's also tempting for youth workers to improve their reputations by getting losers or "burnouts" to join their youth groups and become Christians. If the youth worker is able to get to the teenagers that nobody else can reach, the "punkers" and "druggies," he or she must be especially gifted. In the meantime, the unnoticed kids, the kids who are neither stars *nor* burnouts, get lost. It's easy to ignore those who never win awards or get into trouble. In this highly competitive society, youth workers must learn to affirm the not-too-successful teenagers and make them aware of how special they are.

Brennan Manning, a friend and noted Roman Catholic preacher, told me a story about something that happened to him on a retreat with some nuns. He had conducted a variety of sessions with these nuns and had found them responsive, except for one particular nun. She remained stone faced and unmovable, contributing nothing toward any of the sessions. At the closing gathering, Brennan asked the group, "Would any of you like to share something special that has happened to you this weekend?"

It was then that this withdrawn nun spoke. "Something wonderful happened to me last night," she said. "When I went to bed, I had a dream. And in that dream, I was in a beautiful dance hall. The women were all wearing lovely gowns, and the men were dressed in formal attire. This rather interesting and intense man came and asked me to dance with him, and, as we danced together, I realized that he was Jesus. Halfway through the dance, Jesus leaned over and whispered in my ear. Do you want to know what he said to me?"

The rest of the group sat at the edge of their seats and could hardly wait.

"He said, 'Catherine, I'm crazy about you.' Then he hugged me, and the dream was over."

If there's anything that every struggling teenager needs to hear, it's the good news of how special he or she is to the Lord. If there's anything that a good youth leader should try to communicate to the average kids who come to the church, it's that *Jesus is crazy about them.*

CONSUMERISM AS AN INFECTION AMONG YOUNG PEOPLE

A second cultural value that conditions our young people is consumerism. Consumerism is what drives America these days. Buying is what keeps our economy going and our workers employed. For Americans, buying is a patriotic duty. All of those well-known sayings from *Poor Richard's Almanac* like "A penny saved is a penny earned" have become passé. To keep our economy fueled, we must spend more than we earn, even if it puts us head over heels in debt.

To keep America going, we have to keep buying even though most of us already have everything we need. If we who have everything we need don't keep buying vast quantities of things we do *not* need, then America, as we know it, will grind to a halt. Buying the unnecessary is good for business, and what is good for business supposedly is good for America.

WANTING WHAT WE DON'T NEED

Americans have found ingenious ways to persuade the public—that's us—to buy what we don't need and even to get willingly into debt in the process. First, we've put some of our best minds to work inventing new things that few people ever dreamed would exist. And every year, just before Christmas, we can expect that department stores will display a vast array of new things that were beyond our imaginations a month or so earlier. They may be Cabbage Patch dolls for kids, pocket television sets for dads, or cordless food processors for moms. But one thing is certain—the geniuses of America can be counted on to invent a lot of things we don't need just in time for the Christmas splurge.

When I was a boy, I was always rather content with my possessions until the Sears catalog arrived. Every year, it seemed to get to my house about a month and a half before Christmas. I remember turning through the pages and coming across a host of newfangled inventions and toys that were beyond my wildest imagination. They were usually beyond my parents' budget too. But once having seen them, I knew I had to have them. And if they weren't under the tree on Christmas morning, I knew I would be miserable. Wanting what I didn't need came naturally to me, as it does to most Americans.

Through advertising, the Madison Avenue experts delude us into thinking that these things we don't need are essential for our happiness and well-being. The ads they create promise us that the advertised items can deliver all the emotional gratification we could ever desire. For males who have doubts about their masculinity, the ad-makers lead us to believe that Marlboros will make us tough and strong enough to ride the range of the Wild West with the best of cowpunchers. Virginia Slims tell those women who struggle with being assertive that by smoking a cigarette, they can hold up their heads and say to themselves, "You've come a long way, baby." Teenagers learn early on that certain cars are supposed to make them sexy and that wearing certain clothes promises to lift their stock on the sex-exchange market. Through these ads and others like them, we easily get the sense that all our needs for affirmation and identity can be secured if only we buy the right things.

Teenagers in such a society are molded into consumers. But let's be clear: Our consumer-oriented young people are *not* old-fashioned materialists. They don't buy the things that they do simply because they desire the gratification of physical appetites. On the contrary, our teenage consumers buy what they do because of the deep spiritual hungers of their hearts and souls. They buy certain goods because they long for the love that those who possess the things are supposed to enjoy. They want clothes because the media manipulate them into thinking that their sexual identities will be firmly established and that they will be validated as human beings if they wear the right clothes. They buy because our consumer-oriented society has convinced them that buying establishes the fact that they've come of age and know who they are.

All of this is commonly known to us pseudo-intellectual types, but it still must be said. Any valid understanding of young people requires that we have some comprehension of how the media have psychologically conditioned them to crave the endless array of consumer items constantly being invented to keep our American economy alive. We must understand why the artificially created wants generated by Madison Avenue have become more crucial to the psyche of contemporary young people than their basic human needs. They, in Marxist terminology, have become alienated from what they really need. Instead, they have chosen to become persons who *have* to buy the things they really don't need.

INVOLVING STUDENTS IN SACRIFICIAL SERVICE

As a college teacher, I've taken my students to Third World countries, hoping they will experience firsthand the plight of the world's oppressed people. During such visits, my students usually become involved in projects to help alleviate some of the suffering so pervasive in those countries. While doing such things as feeding hungry children, caring for the elderly sick, working alongside poor families to build their housing, and teaching new mothers about good nutrition, my students discover a need basic to human nature—a need they never knew existed within them. They discover that they have a need to help people. They discover they have a need to love the poor sacrificially. They discover that at the core of their personalities they crave to do things for others and to give away what they have.

It isn't only in Third World countries that I've seen young people make such discoveries. Each summer, well over one hundred college-age young people come to work in a special program to serve children who live in the ghettos of Philadelphia. These young people receive no pay. Sometimes they sleep on basement floors in old churches or in run-down storefront houses. They eat food that they cook for themselves, which is by no means up to the standards they're accustomed to at home.

Each day, these young people go out onto the streets of the city and work with some of the most socially disinherited children in America. The workers give and give until they're exhausted, but they are rewarded for their labor. By the end of the summer, most of them have learned what very few people in our consumer-oriented society have the privilege of learning in a lifetime. They learn that it's more blessed to give than to receive. They learn that getting the things society has seduced them into wanting satisfies only artificially created needs. And they learn that this is a very cheap substitute for satisfying the essential and very *real* need to give oneself away in service to others in the name of Christ.

If I were a youth worker in a middle-class church, I would recognize what young people are like in a consumer-oriented society, and I would respond to their socially created character by finding ways to get them involved in sacrificial service. I would make sure that the programs I envisioned for my group would bring them into direct and personal involvement with people they could help. I would work overtime trying to enable them to discover those suppressed human dimensions that crave the fulfillment that comes only from giving in love to others.

Some years ago, I saw a play that depicted the life of Thomas à Becket. In the beginning of the play, Becket, a libertine, enjoys a life of debauchery with his closest friend, the king of England. However, he soon finds himself appointed archbishop of Canterbury, placed in this lofty position of church leadership by his friend, the king, who wanted the spokesman for the church to be a man who would not criticize his wild ways. After being invested with the mantle of spiritual leadership for England, Becket is completely transformed under the weight of his responsibilities. He becomes saintly in his commitment to the service of God. In a scene just before his ordination as archbishop, he gathers the poor into the sanctuary and gives to them all of his earthly possessions. As he moves among them giving away his clothing, jewelry, and accessories, he abruptly stops, turns to the front of the church, and waving his fists at the crucified Jesus on the cross, screams out, "You! You are the only one who knows how easy this is."

Becket had discovered that through our giving we are shaped into the image of Christ. Like Christ, we are gratified only by giving away what we have for the sake of others. Such lessons can be learned only through personal involvement. Thus, all of us who work with young people need to provide experiences that will enable them to discover what they really are and what really will bring them joy.

PERSONAL HAPPINESS

The third cultural factor that has conditioned the behavior and attitudes of American young people has been generated by the practitioners of psychotherapy. I must plead with those who read this—please understand what I *am* saying about this subject and what I *am not* saying. I *am not* saying that all psychotherapy is worthless and detrimental. Personally, I, along with members of my family, have benefited from psychotherapy. I *am not* saying that Christian counselors are unnecessary. To the contrary, I believe we need Christ-centered counseling that helps people, particularly young people, work out the will of God in their lives.

But I *am* concerned that Americans are increasingly buying into some of the "pop" theories of psychotherapy and embracing with religious fervor some of the erroneous principles on which those theories are often based. Robert Bellah and his associates from the University of Southern California have put together a brilliant critique of this tendency in their book, *Habits of the Heart*. Bellah and his colleagues contend that psychotherapy has had such a powerful effect on us that one of its values—*expressive individualism*—has become an overriding factor in conditioning our behavior.[3] By expressive individualism, Bellah means the belief that it's the duty of every individual to seek personal happiness and self-actualization.

Commitment to self-realization and personal fulfillment has long been part of the American consciousness. But in the past, the drive for expressive individualism was counterbalanced by a deep sense of civic duty. In earlier times, it was considered a good thing for people to seek the actualization of their potential and to strive to experience the personal ecstasy that results from being all that they can be. But even as they did this, Americans were reminded of the fact that they also had obligations to their families, churches, and communities. There was an acknowledged agreement that when the individual's aspirations for personal happiness would lead to an abandonment of duty to others, personal happiness was to be sacrificed.

In those days, Americans received that message from every quarter. For instance, when Tolstoy gave us his novel

Anna Karénina, we had one more example of the doctrine that those who dared abandon duty for personal happiness, regardless of the circumstances, invited disaster and condemnation. In bygone days, people wept and cheered when they heard the couple who starved in the movie *The Prisoner of Zenda* declare that though they loved each other, they would not marry if marrying would keep her from fulfilling her civic duty. When duty called, people were expected to obey—even at the cost of personal happiness.

Things have changed since World War II, and a good bit of that change has resulted from the popularity of the post-Freudian "pop" theories of many psychotherapists. Some practitioners of this profession have replaced the importance of duty with the importance of personal happiness. Increasingly, some have let it be known that they put the well-being of their individual clients at the top of their list of concerns. When persons come for marriage counseling, many psychotherapists will support the maintenance of the marriage only if it doesn't interfere with the happiness and self-actualization of their client. I've talked with some psychotherapists who have told me that if the marital partner stifles the creativity of a client or if the marriage keeps the client from pursuing a vocation that would allow for personal fulfillment, they would condone divorce. Sacrificing personal happiness, even for the sake of children, isn't part of their value system.

As children come of age in this psychotherapeutic society, they're warned not to allow their parents to own them. Young people are made to believe that they owe it to themselves to be all that they can be, even if in the pursuit of self-actualization they have to hurt their parents. The obligation of personal happiness takes precedence over duty to others. Under this "pop" ideology, kids are urged to do their own thing, to find themselves, and to be themselves at all costs. They're told to read *Jonathan Livingston Seagull* and to imagine themselves, like the hero of the story, as having a

31

primary obligation to transcend anything that would limit them or keep them from exercising all of their powers.[4] Psychotherapy has helped to create a cultural ideology that has led contemporary teenagers to regard personal fulfillment as their highest good.

School guidance counselors influenced by this philosophy of self-actualization often encourage teenagers to choose careers that will provide personal satisfaction. Through personality tests, such counselors often claim to be able to discern which vocational options will best enable their students to live happy and fulfilled lives. While there is some validity in what counselors do, most of them direct students on paths of expressive individualism rather than help them optimize their contribution to others by seeking God's will for their lives. Most counselors do not suggest that duty to family, God, and community be given top priority in choosing a vocation.

I'm not suggesting that we do away with school counselors. I believe we need school counselors to help teenagers sort out the overwhelming number of vocational choices they have. But I am saying that counselors too often elevate expressive individualism as an ultimate value, and this has some negative consequences.

It's interesting to note that when the U.S. Army developed a recent series of television ads to induce young men and women to enlist, the ads were designed to play up to the longing that young people have for expressive individualism rather than to set forth a call to duty. The theme of these ads was, "Be all that you can be—in the Army." Note that the ads made no mention of duty to one's country or obligation to others. Military experience was sold on the basis of how it could help the individual to realize his or her potential and get the most out of life through personal actualization. Civic duty was not part of the picture.

Qualifying words notwithstanding, I'm certain that some will take what I have said as a blanket condemnation of psychotherapy. That is *not* what I intend. As a matter of fact, I find one of the best antidotes to the ethos generated by the psychotherapeutic conditioning of our society in one who is himself a leading contemporary psychotherapist—Ernest Becker.[5]

This neo-Freudian, Pulitzer prize winner convincingly tells us that basic to the character of young people is a craving for heroism. It's Becker's belief that young people have a paradoxical quality to their personalities. He thinks that, on the one hand, young people are very aware of a negative, corruptible side to their personhood. They know, he contends, that there is a side of them that is all too human and is oriented toward decay and death. Against this ugly side of their personhood, Becker argues, there is another side that provides young people with an awareness that they are in the image of God. This duality in their personalities creates inner tensions that must be resolved for their psychological well-being. In an effort to resolve the tensions brought on by their paradoxical nature, teenagers seek a way to affirm both their corruptible humanity and the glorious traits of their divinity. The best answer that they can find, according to Becker, is in heroism.

Heroes, claims Becker, are humans who do things that would be a credit to God. The glory of heroes is that even though they are limited by a corruptible humanity that would tend to make them failures, heroes attempt feats worthy of angels. Hence, in heroism, young people see both sides of their personhood affirmed. I agree with Becker when he tells us that "youth was made for heroism and not for pleasure."[6] I'm convinced that young people are turned on by seemingly impossible challenges. I believe that teenagers are thrilled when the evangelist at a youth convention shouts, "If those of us here totally give ourselves to Jesus, we can change the world!" Teenagers hear in such challenges a call to holy crusades in which they can be knights. They hear in the words of the evangelist a call to undertake what they're led to believe is the greatest cause in human history. They can't help but love the almost fanatical call to take over the world for Jesus.

No wonder Fundamentalist churches get the kids. They tell them that they can be heroes by being witnesses for Christ. These churches send their young people into the highways and byways of life to save a dying world from sin. What could be more heroic? What more need be said to lure them from the seductive suggestions of expressive individualism? To those who try to tell these kids that they should "find themselves," these churches shout, "Whoever tries to find himself will lose himself. But whoever is willing to lose himself in the cause of the gospel will find himself."

Perhaps more sophisticated people would want young people to be propagators of a more holistic gospel than one that appears limited to personal evangelism. But the cry has gotten young people to look beyond themselves, and that has to be regarded as some kind of good news.

2 Youth Subcultures

Within our larger American culture, we find smaller subcultures, among them youth subcultures. These youth subcultures are systems of values, beliefs, behavior patterns, and language that enable teenagers to form differentiated sectors of our society. These subcultures provide particular world views to all who are assimilated into their collective mindsets. Morality, attitudes toward the adult world, and even attitudes toward God are established within them as social facts.[1]

Youth subcultures are pervasive; few people escape their conditioning influences. Television, movies, disc jockeys, and stereo records as well as everyday peer relationships conspire to establish the subculture's mindset in teenagers everywhere. Any who don't accept the role definitions ascribed to them by subcultural systems are labeled "nerds" and usually are ostracized as deviants. Across America, young people are socialized into subcultures and are forced to conform to the lifestyles these subcultures prescribe.

EDWARD BANFIELD AND THE TIME PERCEPTIONS OF SUBCULTURES

One of the most subtle and yet most important ways that subcultures are established is through time perceptions. According to Harvard professor Edward Banfield, a given subculture prescribes its own particular sense of time for those who are socialized into it.[2] Banfield claims that what is of crucial significance is how far into the future people are acculturated to imagine themselves realistically. He says that some subcultures establish time perceptions that allow people to think far ahead and to have images in their minds of what life will be like for them. Other subcultures condition people so that nothing is real to them except what is immediately present.

It is Banfield's theory that the more real the future is to people, the more they'll be willing to make present sacrifices to enjoy future rewards. This means, for instance, that young people will make the sacrifices in time and energy to do well in school if they can picture the benefits they'll enjoy years later as a result of getting a good education. Those who fail in school, then, aren't necessarily stupid—they simply may be unable to envision what they might be able to become in the future. They fail, says Banfield, because the "sweet by and by" in which they are supposed to reap the benefits of hard work is not real enough to warrant concerted effort. Most failures are people for whom only the here and now is real. They are the ones who aren't about to give up the pleasures of the present for some deferred gratification in a future they can't even conceptualize.

Put simply, when a subculture conditions people to see the distant future as something very real, it prepares them to make present sacrifices that will have a future payoff. And when a subculture conditions people to view only the here and now as real, it sets them up to be self-indulgent pleasure seekers who will squander their opportunities for a better life.

To say that Banfield's theories are controversial is an understatement. When he was on the faculty of the University of Pennsylvania some years ago, students demonstrated against him. However, in the years since he left Pennsylvania and returned to Harvard, I've become particularly interested in how his theories apply to the American youth subcultures and how they might explain the way in which teenagers are conditioned by their orientations to time and the future.

As I used Banfield's theory in my analysis of the American youth subcultures, I made some interesting observations. On the one hand, I noticed that for a significant proportion of American teenagers, time perception is becoming increasingly confined to the present. For instance, as I talked to some of the teenagers who are part of the punk-rock scene, I sensed that for them there is no tomorrow. When I asked them if they had considered the long-range results of the lifestyle they've adopted, they told me they didn't think about such things. The "punkers" I talked to literally took no thought for tomorrow. They had no vocational plans, and they had no idea what they might want to be a decade or two from now.

They were enmeshed in a world of rock music, and their primary television fare was the videos on MTV. They seemed oblivious to anything or anybody beyond the little world that they and their friends had created for themselves. Not only was the future unreal to them, but those who were not a part of their circle of punkers were not real either. When I asked a teenage girl whose hair was shaved and dyed into a purple Mohawk how she thought her mother felt about her outrageous hairdo, she simply told me she had never really thought about it. All that mattered to her, she told me, was what her *immediate* circle of fellow punkers thought. She had no thought about marriage. Sex for her was something she was doing here and now. She had no thought of going back to school. She saw no point to school. She was part of a subculture that had compressed time into the present, and she was living out the consequences of being a part of that subculture.

But there is another, very different group of teenagers for whom time is becoming more and more extended. When I talk to young people in this group, I find that they are committed to a future that seems to be posited many years ahead. At ages as young as sixteen, members of this latter group talk not only of completing college but also of completing graduate school. They talk about getting married at ages much later than the old established norms of twenty-one years of age for females and twenty-four years of age for males. These young people seem increasingly success oriented, and they take being called "yuppies in the making" as a compliment.

A POLARITY OF SUBCULTURES

After much reflection on these two conflicting pictures of contemporary teenagers, I realized that America had not one, but two youth subcultures and that these two subcultures are polarizing the teenage population. It became increasingly clear to me that over the next few years, American young people will become increasingly identified with one or the other of these two poles-apart subcultures. One group is increasingly focused on the here and now, while the other is intent on a future that is very real to them. This latter group may go to rock concerts and even allow their dress styles to be somewhat influenced by those in the former group, but they aren't even marginal members of what I call the "punk rock sector" of the youth culture. These future-oriented teenagers, full of ambition, are ready to make all kinds of sacrifices that will assure them of a great big, beautiful tomorrow.

When teenagers enter the typical suburban high school, they are faced with an existential decision. They must decide to which subculture they will yield themselves. I say it's an existential decision because, strange as it may seem, there seems to be no rhyme nor reason as to where they eventually end up. I wish I could say that the experiences of their early childhood predispose them to choose one subculture over the other, but to be honest, I don't see a correlation between their preadolescent rearing and the subculture they choose. I've watched teenagers reared in family settings that should have oriented them to be upwardly mobile WASPs, choose to be punk rockers.[3] I've also seen teenagers whose background in no way oriented them toward a yuppie lifestyle choose to belong to the subculture of future-oriented achievers.

I don't want to suggest that I fully understand why teenagers become either punkers or yuppies. The important point is that *two subcultures* are emerging and that American teenagers will tend to move toward one or the other. However, very few "pure types" are found at either end of the spectrum.[4] Instead, most young people establish themselves between the two poles and allow the values of the pole closest to them to mold their attitudes toward life.

Once teenagers choose the subculture to which they want to belong, parents are often at a loss to do anything. Some parents relocate, thinking that if they get their children into another school or another neighborhood, they'll escape from the apparently undesirable subculture. What usually happens, however, is that their children seek out friends who are into the same subculture as the friends they had before the move.

APPEALING TO THE TWO TYPES

If my perspectives on the youth culture are correct, the prospects for youth workers are very challenging. On the one hand, they must make an appeal to the punkers who are committed to nothing beyond the sensate experiences of the present. On the other hand, they're faced with what I think is the even more difficult task of calling an intensely ambitious, yuppie-oriented, youth subculture to consider the fatality of their aspirations and to choose instead to live for the things of God. Needless to say, the old bag of tricks that youth workers have traditionally used won't work in appealing to either of these groups. To do an adequate job with either group, youth work may need to become more specialized, with some youth workers trained to appeal to one subculture and some to the other.

MINISTERING TO PUNK ROCKERS

Teenagers who have accepted the value orientation of the punk-rock subculture may have a great affinity for the Pentecostal/charismatic type of Christianity. First, they are attracted to its orientation to the present. Craving immediate sensate experiences, punk rockers are attracted by the charismatics' focus on the immediacy of God's blessings: "ecstasy in the Spirit," healings, and physical wholeness can be had here and now; there's no need to wait for heaven.

Second, punk-rock types find charismatic Christianity somewhat anti-cultural and defiant toward the beliefs and values of the dominant cultural system. The embracing of the miraculous, so much a part of charismatic Christianity, flies in the face of the normative mindset of our scientifically oriented culture. What the world finds unusual becomes routine when charismatic Christians gather for worship. Their healings, prophecies, and speaking in tongues all defy the logic of the typical American middle-class culture. It's easy to see how black-clad punkers in their surrealist face makeup can easily identify with a brand of Christianity that mocks the ways of the world.

Joining the charismatic movement doesn't ask punkers to become what they are not. Their dress styles are not condemned. They can attend Sunday worship attired in ways that would be totally unacceptable to some mainstream churches. Furthermore, their music has a place in charismatic Christianity, where Christian bands play rock music to the glory of God. This music seems strange to straight types like me. Some people consider it outrageous. But this music provides punkers with a medium for their religious expression.

Recently, I was asked to speak at a Jesus festival. This festival, like many others held across the nation, was a Christian version of the outdoor rock concerts so common in the 1960s. When I got to the grounds, I wondered how a fifty-two-year-old, bald-headed sociologist had ever gotten to be the speaker for this crowd of over 30,000 people. While all kinds of young people were present, those most evident were the representatives of the punk-rock subculture. I had the feeling that I had dropped in on an AC/DC concert rather than a religious festival.

Taking the stage just before I spoke was a musical group called the Rez Band. Their music was not from my world, to say the least. Their antics seemed to be "off the wall." I was sure this band had nothing to do with true Christianity. Yet, as they played, I sensed something happening to the crowd. They were involved with the music on stage, just as I expected them to be. The intense energy in the band's performance was also something I had expected.

What I had *not* expected was that something *holy* was going on. I don't know how else to say it except by using the word "holy." The punk-rock types in the crowd were gyrating to the band's drum beats, but their motions seemed devoid of the orgiastic eroticism that I had been led to expect from such music. Something Christian was happening. When the members of the band gave their testimonies of what the Holy Spirit was doing for them, the crowd cheered them with wild enthusiasm. And when the leader of the band asked for people who wanted to be filled with the Holy Spirit to come forward, literally hundreds came. As I looked on, I realized that God was at work, and through this band and its rock music he was appealing to a group of young people who belonged to a subculture that I had thought it impossible to penetrate with the gospel.

Since that Jesus festival, I've been to a number of charismatic gatherings and churches with large numbers of punk teenagers in their congregations. These young people have not abandoned their cultural lifestyle but apparently have learned how to express love for God and to live out biblical morality within its parameters. It just may be that reaching and ministering to those in the emerging punk-rock subculture is a special calling that God has given to the charismatic movement. Even those on the fringe of the punk-rock subculture may find a validation of their personhood and spiritual renewal in Pentecostal Christianity.

MINISTERING TO YUPPIES

When it comes to the *other* subculture—the adolescent yuppie—youth workers probably face their greatest frustrations. The future orientation of those who are socialized into the yuppie time-consciousness usually makes them a delight to their parents. In so many ways these teenagers are becoming everything that their parents want them to be. They're willing to study hard, sacrifice the pleasures that might be theirs in the present, and live out life according to the mores of the ruling establishment. These young people believe that if they do the things they're supposed to do, they'll find a pot of gold somewhere over the rainbow. For teenagers buying into this subculture, the future not only is very real but also the place they live psychologically. They're convinced that the sacrifices of time and energy required to excel in school will pay off with glorious rewards in the future.

Some people smile benevolently at such a description and say that this type of young person is "just what the doctor ordered" for America. Probably the businessmen down at "the club" puff on their cigars and comfortably assure themselves that the universities are finally getting rid of those counter-cultural "long hairs" who made such a mess of things during the '60s.

This generation of yuppies, however, may not be as healthy a lot as the bourgeois elite would like to think. An article in *Fortune* magazine, "On a Fast Track to the Good Life," reported that this emerging group of young people was assuming the following set of beliefs and values:[5]

1. Success and fulfillment are the result of financial independence.
2. The abilities and capacities of today's graduates make them vastly superior to the present leaders of large corporations.
3. Corporations should maximize profits, even if that means compromising ethical principles.
4. Career is more important than relationships; children are not essential and marriage is tolerable only if it doesn't interfere with career goals.
5. Loyalty to self is more important than loyalty to others; if a job offering more advancement is available, it is valued over loyalty to an employer or company.

As you read this, you may have some of the same reactions I do. I sense that these young people are incredibly self-centered and materialistic. I believe that such a creedal statement can lead to spiritual and psychological disaster. I can picture a grown-up yuppie as a forty-year-old woman sitting alone in a Jacuzzi, staring blankly across the luxuriously furnished bathroom in her Park Avenue apartment and wondering what went wrong. I can imagine our present-day yuppie as a lonely, well-tanned, middle-aged man standing at the bar of Club Med in the Bahamas and asking himself whether hustling another pick-up into bed is worth the effort. In short, I think that these yuppie types are heading for a future that will betray their hopes for happiness, leaving them hollow, empty people.

It seems obvious what those who minister to teenagers buying into this yuppie subculture should be doing. Their mission, I think, is to try to get these teenagers to reject the yuppie goals and replace them with Christian ones.

If the Charismatic movement seems ideally suited to punk-rock types, then Calvinism may be just the ticket for yuppies. It was Max Weber, the German scholar and one of the founders of modern sociology, who delineated the ways in which there was an elective affinity between Calvinist theology and a commitment to hard work and money making.[6] Our Calvinist ancestors would have appreciated the future-orientation of modern-day yuppies. The old Calvinists would have given their approval to the willingness of these young people to endure deferred gratification in the hopes of gaining future rewards. However, the Calvinists would have admonished our contemporary young people to be committed to another version of the good life. They would have said such things as, "Seek ye first the kingdom of God."

Core to the Calvinistic world view is the doctrine of a "calling." Those who follow after the Geneva reformer believe that before the foundation of the world, God has established a mission or calling for each and every person who was ever to be born. People will be fulfilled and satisfied with life, contend the Calvinists, only to the degree to which they commit themselves to becoming what God has willed for them to be. In most instances, discovering the nature of God's plan is a rational process. Christians are expected to consider how their gifts and talents can be best employed in service for Christ and his church. Accordingly, each person is called to look at the available vocational options and choose the one that offers the best possibility to use his or her gifts to maximize good for other people—exactly the approach that offers the best hope for providing a Christian lifestyle for future-oriented young people who might be enticed by yuppie goals and dreams.

During the course of a school year, I speak at as many as twenty different colleges or universities. Usually, I'm asked to speak to the sociology students, and I enjoy that privilege. But I also want the opportunity to speak to students majoring in business. When I ask to be with business students, my hosts are always a bit surprised. Even at Christian colleges, business students are perceived as people who are working toward personal gain, not a divine mission or calling. The "spiritual" students are expected to major in religion, psychology, social work, or some other course of study that prepares people to help others. But I find a latent spirituality in many business students. I often discover that behind their pretended hard, pragmatic "realism" lies a strain of beautiful Christian idealism.

Generally, when I meet business students, I challenge them to spend their lives in service for the poor. I challenge them to take their business talents and training and go to work among the unemployed in America and in the third world. There is a need, I tell them, for Christian business-people to help impoverished people by creating jobs for them and with them. I explain that they could become "entrepreneurs for biblical justice" by helping poor people organize and run businesses that they themselves can own.[7] I tell them about a man I know who helped poor people in Third World countries start 734 small businesses and cottage industries over a ten-year period and how thousands of people found hope in life because of him. I tell them how they can be like him and how they can spend a lifetime doing work that will have eternal significance.

It's always moving to see the faces of those students as I talk to them. It's not unusual to see tears in some eyes. They're moved with the vision of a future of service. They're challenged by the call to a lifestyle in which the payoff is what they become rather than what they get. They make resolutions that their gifts and talents will be used to optimize good for others. Many seem thrilled at the idea of having what the old Calvinists would have called "a calling."

The things I say to business students can be said to students in other fields as well. Pre-med students can be helped to imagine a future in which they would serve the sick in the slums of Haiti or in remote villages in Africa. Engineering students can be told how they might use their genius to develop the appropriate technology for those who need water in Africa's parched Sahel region or for those who need an inexpensive means for efficient farming in the hills of the Dominican Republic. Potential lawyers can be challenged to become the champions for the oppressed, who can't afford to pay for legal services. All of these yuppie-type young people can be encouraged to dream dreams of how glorious their lives could be. And I urge all of them to have visions of the great people they might become. Whenever I have the chance to say such things, I find that students are irresistibly drawn to futures of sacrificial self-giving.

In Arthur Miller's play *Death of a Salesman,* the main character, Willie Loman, commits suicide. As his wife and his son Biff stand by his graveside, she asks her son, "Why did he do it, Biff? Why did he do it?"

Biff answers, "Ah shucks, Mom, ah shucks! He had all the wrong dreams. He had all the wrong dreams!"

That's what is wrong with yuppie-ism. The orientation of yuppies to the future makes them into diligent stewards of time and talent. Their ambition is a positive virtue, but they have all the wrong dreams. It's the task of youth workers to inspire their young people with the right dreams. That may be a difficult task, but the salvation of a host of teenagers whose orientation to the future makes them easy prey for yuppieism may depend on its being done.

GOD CONCEPTS IN THE YOUTH SUBCULTURES

There's a real danger that the young people in each of these two youth subcultures will generate some very distorted concepts of God. The great French sociologist Emile Durkheim figured out that each group of people who share a collective consciousness tends to create a god in the group's own image. Consequently, we should expect that young people in the punk-rock subculture or the yuppie subculture will generate a deity that incarnates the subculture's own traits and values.

46

THE GOD OF THE PUNK-ROCK SUBCULTURE

The god of the punk-rock subculture probably emerges as one who flouts convention while he defies the social order. This god isn't hung up on the seemingly petty legalism that makes the members of established religion so uptight, and he mocks the hypocrisy of their way of life. The god of the punk-rock subculture isn't so much intent on changing the world into a just and righteous kingdom as he is on creating a world in which people can live and let live. He's a god who lets everybody do his or her own thing as long as nobody gets hurt.

Instinctively and unconsciously, some youth ministers assess the covert theology of the punk-rock subculture and affirm this god who belongs to it. As youth ministers try to be relevant, they sometimes define god in ways that bring cheers from the crowds of teenagers who gather at religious rock festivals. At one Jesus festival, I heard one of the "with it" speakers say something like this:

> What do you think God is like? Do you think he's some kind of wimp who plays up to adults by being their version of a goody-goody? Do you think he's some kind of nerd who doesn't know how to have a good time? Then you're wrong! He's a God who accepts you just like you are. He's a God who thumbs his nose at the straight people who want to put him in their little box. When Jesus was here on earth, he liked parties—they called him a winebibber.

While those in the punk-rock subculture might really "groove" on this deity, we have to ask if the presentation of such a god encourages idolatry. If the punk rockers end up worshiping this god, they probably will end up worshiping a god who is other than the biblical God. In worshiping this deity, they will not be worshiping the God who revealed himself in Jesus, but they will be worshiping none other than themselves. As Durkheim clearly understood, the god created

47

by and for a particular subculture is nothing more than a collective representation of the traits evident in its creators.

THE GOD OF THE YUPPIES

Those who belong to the yuppie subculture are also creating a god in their own image. Yuppies want a god who is a success deity and who promises to bless those who faithfully do what they're supposed to do. Their god must be one who encourages them to imagine glorious materialistic goals and who calls them to exercise the will power needed to reach those goals. Their god must be a rational deity whose ways fit into a glorious plan for good, even if that plan transcends the comprehension of his believers. Yuppies need a god who will make all things work together for good, even if that good will not be known for several years.

I read about a successful pro football player who told a group of teenagers that if Jesus were in their high school, he would be an honor-roll student and an all-star athlete in every sport. Once again, God was being transformed into what the worshipers wanted him to be.

LET GOD BE GOD

This tendency to create a god that reflects and affirms what we already know led the apostle Paul to write in Romans,

> Although they claimed to be wise, they became fools and exchanged the glory of the immortal God for images made to look like mortal man and birds and animals and reptiles. . . . They exchanged the truth of God for a lie, and worshiped and served created things rather than the Creator—who is forever praised. Amen (Rom. 1:22–23, 25).

Undoubtedly, there's some truth in both of these god concepts. All heresy is partly right, and all idolatries have some validity. I don't want to suggest that God is not a vital, joyful person who wants his joy to be in all of us. Nor do I want to convey that God is unconcerned about people becoming all that they can be as they fully exercise the gifts and talents he gives them. It's just that God is more than the creation of any group. The God who is revealed in Jesus is more than an affirmation of what we are—he also reminds us of what we ought to become and what we have so far failed to become. While we all need affirmation from God, we also need him to challenge us to become new creatures in *his* image, as that image is revealed through Scripture.

Biblically faithful youth workers will present to teenagers in both subcultures a Jesus that both affirms the best that is in them and yet calls them to be other than they are as they see the *fullness* of God in Christ Jesus. Each subculture conditions those who are in it to see God "through a glass darkly" and to know him only "in part."[8] As much as possible, youth workers should do their best to teach the whole message of the Word of God so that young people in both subcultures will know what they're called to become instead of believing in gods that only affirm what they already are.

3 Primary Groups and Con Jobs

HOW PRIMARY GROUPS WORK

Almost every teenager belongs to what Charles Cooley, an American sociologist, calls a *primary group*—a small circle of friends or associates who interact intensely with him or her almost daily. The members of a primary group provide a reference point for the teenager. In face-to-face encounters with them, the young person establishes a personal identity and patterns of behavior.

The dominant culture may provide some basic values for teenagers, and the particular subculture to which they belong may prescribe their lifestyle. However, the extent to which the social forces of either the culture or the subculture affect a particular teenager is determined by his or her primary group. That close circle of friends will help evaluate for the individual just how much importance should be given to the messages that are being received from outside the primary group. These friends will help the individual to decide the extent to which conformity to the value orientation of the dominant culture or the particular subculture is desirable. They will help the teenager determine just how deeply he or she will get into the lifestyle of the chosen youth subculture. The primary group helps censor all incoming influences, filtering out what it decides is unacceptable and contrary to its own definition of what is "cool."

During his last two years of high school, Fred became part of a primary group that significantly shaped his life. All six guys in the group were good athletes, got fairly good grades, and were good looking. In many ways they were an elite group in the high school they attended.

These boys did everything together. As a group, they became involved in the youth program of a dynamic church in the neighborhood, and that involvement significantly changed them. They accepted the values of the dominant culture, but only as those values were moderated by their primary group. For instance, they weren't as competitive as they might have been. Perhaps several of them could have even won athletic scholarships had they taken sports more seriously. But when it came to excelling in sports, the attitude of this primary group was "no big deal." They looked at sports as a means to have fun, and they were not about to "work" at being superstars. It was the same with academics. Fred scored so well on his college board tests that he earned the title of Merit Scholar. Nevertheless, he seldom made the honor roll at school. His marks were always better than decent, but he tended to do poorly in those courses that didn't particularly interest him.

The members of this primary group had a time-consciousness similar to yuppies. Yet the future orientation that they readily adopted didn't motivate them to go after the kinds of things that characterize the yuppie lifestyle. They didn't buy expensive cars and clothes. They didn't buy into fads.

Since graduating from college, these guys have talked about going to live in an urban slum and developing ministries for poor people. It's obvious that this primary group is able to determine the ways they'll allow themselves to be conditioned by the cultural influences constantly bombarding them from society.

Another young man I know is just as religious as Fred, but he has a very different way of living. Bill was once arrested in a drug bust and was convicted for possession of narcotics. The judge who sentenced him gave him the choice of going to prison or going into a rehabilitation program run by charismatic Christians. He chose the latter alternative, and that decision changed the course of his life.

Bill was taken to a farm in Pennsylvania, and there he was put into a religious routine that led to a traumatic religious conversion. His religious experience was shared with several other former drug users who had gone through a similar kind of conversion. Their common religious experience became the basis for developing a deep sense of camaraderie among them. Three of Bill's friends had some musical talent and formed a Christian rock band. Along with three other new converts, this young man decided to accompany the band when they went out to play at youth gatherings. Eventually the group developed into a "gospel team," with non-musicians giving testimonies and preaching. The ministry of this group has become a full-time job for them. They're constantly traveling around the country, sharing the gospel.

This primary group is composed of young men who share a very truncated time concept. Like punk rockers, they're focused on the present. They don't want to waste their time discussing where they might be in the future. "Now" is important for them. While they don't dress like punkers, their clothes do make them look very much like a motorcycle gang. They're totally indifferent to the consumerism that is part of the consciousness of most Americans. They have no aspirations for greater success. They seem to be perfectly content doing what they're doing.

While this primary group may be oriented toward the values of the punk-rock subculture, its members can filter out what they find unacceptable about that subcultural lifestyle. Actually, they can be quite ferocious in their attack on what punk rockers think and do. They condemn drug users as being under the influences of Satan. They not only condemn the drug use and the promiscuous sex that is so often part of the punk-rock lifestyle, they also condemn rock music itself.

This may appear a bit odd to outsiders, since the group members themselves play rock music. However, they strongly argue that there is a big difference between their music and the music of the world. The music of the world, they say, encourages lust and glorifies drug use, while their music glorifies God and tells people about the joy they've come to know through Christ. Many teenagers have been converted to the Christian faith because of their music.

This gospel team provides a good example of how the influences from the outside can be controlled and modified by a primary group so that its members become a pronounced variant of the subculture with which they would normally be associated. These young people, in accord with biblical definitions, are "in" a particular subculture but not "of" it.

Of course, primary groups can also work against Christianity, and unfortunately, that may be a more common phenomenon. Recently I shared the speaking responsibilities at a Bible conference with a prominent youth evangelist. This man has established a widespread reputation as one who loves Christ, in spite of his wildly counter-cultural lifestyle. The first time I met him, he was wearing motorcycle boots, a denim jacket, and grubby leather trousers. His long hair made him look like a leftover from the '60s (which he probably was). He was a brilliant speaker, and once he started preaching, the audience was readily convinced that his style was real. This forty-eight-year-old man may have appeared to be a middle-aged man trying to patronize the members of a particular subculture, but when I got to know him, I discovered that wasn't the case. This guy was for real. There was nothing phony about him whatsoever.

The best way I can describe him is to say that he strangely embodied some of the prophetic style of the prophet Amos, the intellect of a J. I. Packer, and the mannerisms of Hell's Angels. I would have to say that he proved to be one of the most interesting and unique persons I've ever met.

This unusual man was married and had two teenage children. His children easily identified with their father and adopted his lifestyle, but with significant differences. They had been drawn into a primary group that rejected the Evangelical Christian faith that their father so fervently espoused. Their close friends were deeply immersed in the rock subculture and were frequent drug users. Their primary group reinforced the values of the rock music that came across in the videos on MTV. While they loved their father, they were much more controlled by their primary group than by him. Appeals from other evangelists were unsuccessful. The teenagers were convinced that their dad was the best thing that Christianity had going. But even a dad whom they intensely loved was not able to counter the control that their primary group exercised over them.

CREATING PRIMARY GROUPS

Primary groups don't necessarily form accidentally. They can be deliberately created, and they can be programmed to communicate a particular value system and enforce particular behavior patterns.

This is good news to youth workers, but it's also a great responsibility. From the time young people are fifteen to the time they're twenty-five, they make almost all the major decisions that will shape the rest of their lives. They decide on the person they will marry, whether or not to go to college, and what their vocational choices will be. Most important, they decide on the role that Christ and the church will play in their lives. To leave young people on their own in the face of such decisions is irresponsible. Engineering teenagers into support groups that will provide a loving context in which to work through these concerns seems the ideal way to go.

Charles Cooley said that people tend to become what

55

they think those in their primary groups expect them to be. Cooley believed that primary groups were the most important sociological agencies in molding personality and determining how people will act in their everyday lives.[1] I believe that he was right. This means that youth workers must learn to pay more attention to primary groups and, if possible, learn how to engineer young people into what I have labeled as Christian support groups. Perhaps no challenge in ministering to young people is more important.

My son's life was profoundly affected by a wise and effective church youth leader named Phil Thorne. The primary group that played such a crucial role in Bart's life was Phil's creation. He went out of his way to befriend Bart and the others in his group. He hung out at the high school and often attended sports events to affirm this group of teenagers and to demonstrate his interest in them. One day, he invited Bart's gang to start meeting with him regularly. During those early morning meetings, Phil interjected theological and biblical topics for discussion. Over an extended period of time, this primary group developed a deep sense of belonging and came to share a collective set of Christian values.

THE IMPORTANCE OF CHRISTIAN SUPPORT GROUPS

As a sociologist who is often called on to speak for youth workers, I try to communicate the importance of primary groups in the creation and maintenance of the Christian faith and lifestyle. It's my belief that unless young people experience constant reinforcement through such small groups, they will have little chance of having an ongoing relationship to Christ. The pressures of the dominant culture and influences of the youth subcultures will sooner or later overpower even the most sincere commitments to live like Christians. So often young people will go forward at evangelistic services in response to the invitation to commit themselves to Christ—only to discover later that their commitments were not longlasting. Were those commitments insincere or shallow? No, rather, those commitments were not reinforced. Reinforcement provided by the right kinds of primary groups could have kept them from slipping away from God.

Peter Berger and Thomas Luckmann in their book *The Social Construction of Reality* give a clear picture of how primary groups function and how important they are in maintaining belief systems and associated behavioral expectations.[2] Berger and Luckmann refer to small primary groups as *plausibility structures*. They make it clear that young people will be able to sustain beliefs that are at odds with the dominant societal systems only if their deviant beliefs are constantly revitalized by a primary group. Only by having intimate interaction with close friends who affirm their beliefs and assure them that their chosen way of life is not crazy will young people have the courage and fortitude to carry out their commitments. What is real and true, say Berger and Luckmann, is what the primary group assures them is real and true.

For young people who don't experience the support of a primary group of believers, Christianity can easily become implausible and a cast-off religion. Once having lost their faith, such young people will wonder how they ever believed "that stuff" in the first place. When they're once again swallowed up by the dominant social forces, it becomes very difficult to get them back into the Christian faith because they think what they formerly believed was nothing more than the result of group manipulation or a form of temporary stupidity. That may be why the writer of the epistle of the Hebrews wrote:

> It is impossible for those who have once been enlightened, who have tasted the heavenly gift, who have shared in the Holy Spirit, who have tasted the goodness of the word of God and the powers of the coming age, if

57

they fall away, to be brought back to repentance, because to their loss they are crucifying the Son of God all over again and subjecting him to public disgrace (Heb. 6:4–6).

WHAT CHRISTIAN SUPPORT GROUPS ACCOMPLISH

What is true for young people is true for everyone. I, myself, belong to a four-member primary group that meets regularly. We provide mutual encouragement as each of us tries to live out the Christian faith. Our meetings are by no means always "heavy," although our discussions sometimes get fairly deep. Most of the time, our get-togethers are a time of fun and catching up with each other. However, in times of trouble, each of us finds precious consolation from this support group. When important decisions must be made, the support group provides great help in evaluating the options.

About twenty years ago, I founded a missionary organization, the Evangelical Association for the Promotion of Education, which promotes a variety of missionary programs among poor people both in the United States and in third-world countries. The members of my support group are a vital part of EAPE. And because this organization is the primary means through which I seek to serve Christ, these friends are my partners in Christian mission. To be perfectly frank, without the help of my support group, I would have messed up my life by this time. I also know that without them my ministry would be in a state of chaos. My support group is second only to my wife in helping me in my walk with Christ.

Support groups are positive for many reasons. First, my support group provides an environment in which God can shape me. In my experience, something quite spiritually mysterious can occur in the context of intensive, small-group interaction. I have experienced times of deep spiritual renewal while enjoying Christian fellowship (koinonia, for the more theologically sophisticated). I can say without hesitation that in the context of my support group, I have experienced a filling of the Holy Spirit. It's not that such times of spiritual renewal have been marked by the manifestation of some spiritual gifts such as speaking in tongues (although I have no reason to doubt that such things happen under the influence of the Holy Spirit) but that I have experienced empowerment and joy. On those special occasions when the Holy Spirit is particularly evident (and I don't want to suggest that these times occur on schedule or even with fair regularity) I find that all religious doubts are vanquished and that there is a splendid sense of psychological exhilaration.

M. Scott Peck, in his book *The Different Drum,* suggests that what I am experiencing at these times is "community."[3] Insofar as Peck, who writes from a Christian perspective, claims that community is a spiritual experience, I agree with him. Yet, there's more going on here than just community (as sacred as that is). What I'm experiencing at such times might be better labeled *communion.* I didn't come up with that particular nomenclature on my own. Herman Schmalenbach, a contemporary German scholar in the field of the sociology of religion, suggested that title for me.[4] Schmalenbach observed that in certain religious gatherings, an extraordinary spiritual sharing can give participants an overwhelming sense of oneness and a wonderful sense of joy that renders them a bit giddy. This description comes close to what I've experienced in those special times with my support group.

I believe most people have an intense hunger for such ecstatic experiences and that these experiences are essential validations of God's presence with us. I'm not suggesting that support groups are the only means for gaining these kinds of spiritual experiences, but I do say that for me, the theophanies in which the Holy Spirit has taken the dryness of my soul away have come through this means.

Second, my support group has helped me by providing insights and corrections for the things that are wrong in my life. My friends hold me accountable for what I do and don't do. They check on whether or not I'm regularly reading Scripture and consistently praying. They let me know when they discern unchristian traits developing in my personality. They correct me when I get sucked into behavior patterns that might be destructive.

I have a strong tendency to overextend myself by taking more speaking engagements than any sane person should. My support group keeps that tendency from working itself out into a speaking schedule that would break me. I have a great weakness when people ask me to do things that I really shouldn't be doing (i.e., such as serving on committees and boards). My friends usually insist that I get out of these responsibilities so that I can pay attention to the things upon which I ought to be focusing.

Third, my support group helps me discern God's will. My life involves lots of decisions—decisions about vocational choices, decisions about programs for our missionary organization, decisions about personal concerns with my children, or decisions about my relationship to my wife. When I was younger, I had far too little help with making decisions and often depended on hunches and instincts, which sometimes got me into trouble. Now I often turn to my support group for help. They listen to the decisions I need to make, and they help me sort out the alternatives. They pray for me and point me to appropriate Scripture passages.

In working through decisions or troublesome issues, I wait for a concensus to emerge out of our discussions. I believe that when we've talked and prayed ourselves into a singleness of mind, we have discovered God's will. The Book of Acts tells us that the early church discovered the will of God this way. Those first-century Christians assumed that when they were together and of one accord, they were in line with the leading of the Holy Spirit (Acts 5:12; 15:25). We also believe we are following the direction of Christ, who let us know that if we be agreed on anything, he will enter into it and make it happen (Matthew 18:19). We are convinced that we are responding to the promise of the Lord who told us that, when two or three gather together in his name, his leading will be felt in a special way (Matthew 18:20).

HOW TO CREATE CHRISTIAN SUPPORT GROUPS

Young people need to belong to support groups that can do for them what my group does for me. They need help in trying to figure out what God wants them to do with their lives. Almost every time I lead a youth retreat, I'm confronted by several earnest teenagers, each of whom inevitably asks, "How can I figure out the will of God for my life?" I suggest that the inquiring teenager put together a support group and learn to work through the serious concerns of life with the help of that group. I tell them how my support group works for me and suggest ways that they can set up a support group of their own.

Step 1: Take the initiative. Don't wait for a group to "happen." Ask a Christian your own age and sex if he or she would meet with you for a few hours each week so that the two of you can help each other live out the Christian life. I emphasize that the partner should be of the same sex so that the expected intimacy that develops out of the relationship doesn't get messed up by sexual turn-ons. Another reason is that often the problems that have to be worked through in living a Christian life involve overcoming sexual temptations. Consequently, it's easier to talk about such things with friends of the same sex.

Step 2: Invite a few other people to join your group. Pick people you would naturally have as friends. If you choose kids you like, you've minimized the difficulties for building a deep sense of community. Pray before making your choices, just as Jesus did before he picked the men who

61

would be his closest friends. I recommend a group size of four people.

Step 3: Make a covenant to meet at least once a week. A covenant is a very serious promise. Support groups don't work unless commitment to them is high. You need at least a couple of hours each time you meet so that you don't feel rushed.

The format of your group can vary according to the needs of your group. Our group usually works through a book of the Bible over the course of a few months, each week focusing on one passage and sharing ideas or insights about what the Lord may be trying to say to each of us in that passage. And we try to spend time each week praying for each other. We leave room for spontaneity in the format for the get-together. Sometimes when one of the guys in my support group has a special problem, we do nothing else but deal with what's on his mind. And give yourselves time; community doesn't develop in two or three weeks. But over the months, you'll learn to trust and depend on each other for support.

CREATING OUR SELVES

THE SELF AS A CON JOB

We've already concluded that teenagers act the way they do because of their social environment—their culture, subculture, and the censoring controls of their primary groups. But beyond these influences is the influence of the young person's self-image.

Erving Goffman, a man proven to be one of the most significant social theorists of the last two decades, gives us some help in our attempt to understand how teenagers decide how they will act. In his book *The Presentation of Self in Everyday Life* Goffman says, with some admiration, that the teenager is a kind of con artist who attempts to manipulate people in order to get desired responses. A teenager, says

Goffman, has no single self-image but instead is constantly poised to create the kind of self-image that best serves his or her purposes in a given situation.[5]

Out of learned knowledge and past experiences, the teenager is able to create a self for almost any occasion. For instance, if a guy is interested in getting a particular girl to notice him, he won't make his move until he's figured out what kind of guy he thinks she'll like. Then he'll project for her a self that is just what she had in mind for a date.

Of course he's conning her. The self that he's presenting isn't real; it's made up just for the occasion. And she's probably doing the same thing to him. The ensuing date will be between two con artists, each pretending to be what the other wants in a date. Should the date lead to a serious relationship and eventually to marriage, both will discover that they have been conned.

The teenager Goffman envisions has the ability to construct a variety of selves and is always ready to create an appropriate one for whomever he or she is trying to impress. In each situation, the teenager is trying to get something. In order to get what he or she wants, the person readily constructs the self that will serve that goal. For instance, a young man in school can present himself as a student who's trying hard to learn, if that's what it takes to get a good grade. Or in church he can construct a religious self that will get him elected president of the youth fellowship group, if that's the goal. The teenager, says Goffman, is an actor who can play whatever role the social script requires.

What is this con artist really like? What lies behind the false self he or she assumes in the manipulative games? What is this person's essential self? Goffman grimly suggests that there may be no essential self at the core of the teenager's being.[6] It may be that this con artist is nothing more than the sum total of all the con jobs that he or she has learned to play. This mysterious teenager may be without any core identity at all. As unpleasant as that prospect is, I believe it to be correct. Some of the existentialist philosophers (i.e., Jean Paul Sartre, author of *Being and Nothingness*) have said much the same thing.

I believe that every teenager is working overtime to escape from this truth. Each is trying to get away from the sense that beneath all the presentations of self lies an abyss of nothingness. This awareness that there is no essential identity creates what Søren Kierkegaard, the nineteenth-century Danish philosopher, called *angst*. We can roughly translate this as anxiety. This anxiety is difficult for the teenager to handle and, if it gets to be too much to endure, the troubled young people may resort to suicide. However, most do not go to that extreme; they simply become sullen and withdrawn, fearing the question, "What are you going to *be* when you get out of school?"

CHOOSING A LIFESTYLE

Trying to escape the sense of nothingness that lies beneath the conning roles, the teenager may make some kind of commitment. The imaginary young man I just described might decide that he's tired of playing games with people. He may be exhausted with his constant role changing. And because of that, he might choose one particular self and identify with it completely. He may pick a presentation of self that he had constructed for conning purposes and say to himself, "That's going to be me." Once such a commitment is made, the teenager becomes "a man for all seasons." He becomes consistent. His lifestyle becomes somewhat fixed.

Perhaps the guy in question feels accepted by a group of teenagers who are "artsy." These young people love classical music and frequently go to art museums. They have an attitude of superiority toward the other kids in the high school. He likes that because it gives him a feeling of superiority too. From this point on, everything about him will be in harmony with the self that belongs to that group. His dress, his conversation, the TV shows he watches, the way he spends his money, the kind of church he goes to, and even the kind of girl he dates will all be conditioned by his choice. He won't change when he's with people who are different. He won't play different roles for different groups as he once did. He'll have overcome what David Riesman called "other-direction." He has established an identity. He has decided who he is. His primary group accepts and affirms his chosen identity. He, in collusion with the others in his primary group, will determine which societal values will be taken seriously and which will be ignored. Together they'll decide what factors in their social environment can contribute to their efforts to construct the kinds of lives they want to live. Once having made this commitment, all else follows in a rational, predictable pattern.

If our hypothetical teenager follows this pattern, his parents probably will be pleased and proud. However, the young man we have imagined is just as likely to follow another route. He may find that he feels most comfortable with the identity of a social rebel. Perhaps he feels good being a punk rocker. If such is the case, his decision will establish what he will be like in all other social situations and settings. Probably, to his parents' dismay, he'll be that way at home as well as when he's out with the primary group that affirms and revitalizes his commitment.

CREATING A SELF THROUGH CHRISTIAN COMMITMENT

Earlier, I emphasized an important truth: that the primary group is important in determining how cultural values and patterns will affect the individual teenager. Now I want to point out another truth, one that may seem almost contradictory to the first: that the teenager need not be a social product. While most submit to what groups do to them, there are those who are empowered to control their own destinies. Yes, teenagers are influenced by groups—but, in the end, only to the extent they choose to be. After all is said and done, each teenager has a personal will and can assert that will against all the influences and subcultures that primary groups exercise on him or her. While the teenager is highly impressed by social factors, we must not assume that these forces ultimately *determine* what he or she will become. While most are conditioned by the groups they live with from day to day, there are some who, by self assertion, challenge social forces to establish their own identities. I believe that, with God's help, a teenager can affirm an identity in Christ. They can then join with others who have made a similar commitment, so that they might mutually reinforce their chosen identities.

This is what makes youth ministry so exciting. Youth workers deal with people at one of the most crucial times in life—the time when identities are chosen. They interact with young people during the periods of development when teenagers are most free to define themselves in opposition to what societal forces would make them to be. It's possible, although unlikely, for people to decide later in life that the identities they've chosen for themselves are erroneous or unworthy of them. I say that it's unlikely because, generally, even though adults may modify their lifestyles, they still organize their decisions and lifestyles around the commitments they made during their teenage years. Conversions are possible later on in life (that's why the gospel means "good news"), but they come hard. Therefore, it's wise to call for Christian commitment before commitments to any other identities are made.

Youth workers have the exciting opportunity to help teenagers avoid a lot of grief in the years that lie ahead. By presenting God as a God of grace and love, youth workers will help teenagers be attracted to them and feel "at home" with them. Furthermore, youth workers must convince teenagers that the Christian life is an adventure that offers a greater sense of aliveness and joy than any alternative presented by the world. If teenagers are to choose Christ, they must be convinced that the life he offers is the only one worth living. Christianity, therefore, must not be presented simply as a set of propositional truths that should be accepted in order to be saved and go to heaven. It must be presented as a total lifestyle and as a mission that demands complete self-giving. Christianity must involve a decision about what teenagers will do with the rest of their lives. It should be the essence of their definitions of self.

If this generation of teenagers is lost to the church, it will be not because we demanded too much from them but because we demanded too little. We must call teenagers into an identity in Christ. We must invite them to be born again into a lifestyle that conforms to God's expectations. We must tell them to accept from society only those values that can help them live out their new identities with maximum effectiveness. Once they have decided for Christ, we must urge them to form support groups that will strengthen them against the forces that can easily overwhelm them and destroy their newly found identities. We must be sure that they're not naïve about the opposition they will face. We must remind them that

> our struggle is not against flesh and blood, but against the rulers, against the authorities, against the powers of this dark world and against the spiritual forces of evil in the heavenly realms (Eph. 6:12).

Youth work is indeed a noble vocation!

4 The Death of Traditional Parenthood

Today's parents are bewildered and not quite sure how to do the job. Confused about their role, they look to experts, hoping for some clear definitions. No such luck. The "experts" are as confused as the parents.

Social scientists offer a conflicting variety of options for parents to follow. Opinions about even the most basic aspects of parenting change dramatically from one year to the next. For instance, a sign in the window of a Washington toy shop recently listed the changing advice that child specialists have given about discipline over the past sixty years:

1920—spank them
1930—deprive them
1940—ignore them
1950—reason with them
1960—love them
1970—spank them lovingly
1980—to hell with them

NO HELP FROM PSYCHOLOGY

Harry Stack Sullivan, the founder of modern social-work practice, predicted that by 1980, child rearing would be reduced to a science. Professionals in the field of child psychology would give precise direction to parents. His optimism was misguided. While specialists offer many theories and proposals, an endless array of books, countless seminars, and a constant barrage of television talk shows—

all of which seek to inform and educate parents—there is no consensus.

The basic theme of psychological advice givers is that parents are responsible for everything that goes wrong with their children. Consequently, most parents are on guilt trips. They hold themselves personally responsible for their children's maladjustments. In reality, parents take far too much blame for the problems of their children, and they take far too much credit when their children turn out well. The environment parents create for children is important but doesn't necessarily determine how a child turns out.

On my own TV show I once interviewed a prominent child psychologist who said categorically: "All problems of children and teenagers originate with their parents." I disagreed, indicating that God created two biologically perfect children, placed them in a perfect environment, and yet both rebelled and ruined their lives.

Perhaps the best critique of the failures of modern psychology in the field of child rearing can be found in Christopher Lasch's book *A Haven in a Heartless World*. Lasch not only points out the failures of the "experts" and the undeserved guilt they place on parents, but he also indicates societal factors that are far more important than parental influence in determining the character of children. These other factors need careful attention and analysis by youth workers.

GET READY FOR *GESELLSCHAFT*

Harvard sociologist David Reisman, in his now-classic book *The Lonely Crowd,* argued that the confusion about parent roles lies in the nature of society and the demands it places on those who are socialized into its system. Reisman pointed out that modern-day children are raised in what sociologists call a *gesellschaft,* a social system in which people change groups each time they change functions.[1] Family activities are carried out in a group that is distinct from the work group, and the work group is likely to be composed of people different from those met in the play group, who in turn will be different from those in the religious group.

Reisman suggested that acceptance into these groups is not a given. In each case, individuals must engineer acceptance. According to Reisman, fitting into different groups effectively requires that children have *other-directed personalities*.[2] Such children have what he calls "social antennae," which enable them to pick up what any particular group expects in the way of social behavior.

The ability to be accepted readily by new groups is something that *gesellschaft* parents hope to develop in their children. Whereas parents in the nineteenth century sought to produce *inner-directed* children who were committed to individualistic success, contemporary parents seek to produce children who are experts in public relations.

An unfortunate result of the *gesellschaft* system is that kids live under the dictatorship of a variety of peer groups. They know that the social acceptance they've worked so hard to engineer can be taken from them by one mistake. They can lose their status by tripping in the cafeteria, saying something that is considered "dumb," holding a viewpoint that is considered ludicrous, or wearing the wrong clothes. They walk on tiptoe, fearing that they might do or say something that will bring scorn on them. They lose their spontaneity because they would rather do nothing at all than risk doing something that might lead to rejection.

Parents are prone to brag about the other-directedness of their children. "My kids adapt easily. You can put them with new people, and they fit right in." Popularity is the mark of success for children, according to *gesellschaft* parents, and they see their primary task as training their children in the techniques of gaining this popularity.

I find it interesting that young people often are criticized for being too adaptable. Parents ridicule them for dressing, talking, and acting like their peers. The church condemns these other-directed young people for "conforming to the world." Yet, it is the other-directed personality, with all of its propensities for adaptability and conformity, that parents often deliberately encourage.

Once other-directedness is defined as a virtue to be encouraged in children, the problems associated with parenthood become arduous, if not impossible. Do parents *know* what behavior will make their children popular? Do parents *know* the popular musical tastes, dating styles, and sexual norms? The answer to such questions is obviously no. How could they know? The world is changing too quickly for parents to keep up with fashion. Few parents are capable of telling their children what is considered "cool" by their children's peers. In short, parents have nothing to *teach* their children about what is most important in modern society. They have no knowledge to dispense with authority. Therefore their children have no reason to respect the parents' opinions about the most important childhood challenge: how to gain acceptance and popularity.

WHO RUNS THE MODERN FAMILY?

The patriarchal family outlined in Scripture is difficult to maintain in a modern, urban, industrial society. It was easy for fathers to be rulers of domestic life in the pre-industrial, agrarian era because men were home most of the time. Farmers worked at home, and they lived out their days in the company of the family members. Men could value their families because they were always with them.

In today's urban, industrial society, however, the father is absent from the home for most of each working day. Leaving home at seven in the morning, he's usually gone until at least six o'clock in the evening. Consequently, the father has lost his position of control in the family, not because the feminist movement has required it, but because it has become impossible to control his household when he's absent most of the time.

In the absence of the father, it would seem that the mother would take over the reins of control; she seems to be the heir apparent. And it might have been a good thing if she had taken control. But it didn't work out that way.

Women in America have been victimized by the cult of *Momism.* Our culture has perpetuated a belief that the primary function of a mother is to be a "love machine." Mothers believe that the psychological health of their children is directly related to the love that grows up between mother and child. However, it's difficult to be loved and to exercise rule at the same time. Discipline elicits antagonism, and mothers who are desperate to be loved are afraid to be disciplinarians. They fear that punishing their children will destroy their own capacity to be love machines. The typical mother latently senses that she must choose to be *either* a recipient of love *or* a strong leader/disciplinarian, and she finds conflict between these roles. Any survey of relationships between mothers and children quickly shows what role American mothers have chosen. They have decided to be loved.

If the father can't rule the home because he's not there and if the mother is afraid to rule for fear her children won't love her, one might ask, "Who *does* rule the typical American middle-class family?" The answer is, the children do. It is Kiddie City out there in the WASP suburbs of America. We have developed the first filio-centric family system in human history. Anyone who has observed children controlling their parents in supermarkets and department stores will verify this fact. School teachers complain that when children misbehave, it does little good to report them to their parents because children so control their parents that children get their parents to side with them against the teachers.

Erik Erikson, one of the leaders in the field of child development studies, claims that when children assume control of their own lives, they often become emotionally destabilized. Erikson claims that many youngsters are emotionally disturbed because they are making decisions that they shouldn't be making until they've entered a more advanced stage of social development.[3]

TV'S DEVASTATING IMPACT

Television must also be cited as a major factor contributing to the difficulty of modern parenting. This isn't surprising when we consider the fact that the average child watches television five hours a day. Television dominates the consciousness of young people.

Television's most direct influence on parenting comes from its ability to define what children should expect of parents. Growing up watching situational comedies from *Leave It to Beaver* to *The Cosby Show*, children and teenagers see an array of television parents who become models to which their own parents are expected to conform. TV parents are never exhausted after a day's work. They are never tense and irritable. They are always wise and extremely fair. The parents on television shows are open to learn what the youth culture is all about. They are gentle and kind when their children have problems. They are able to resolve any dilemma in twenty-four minutes. And most of all, they are completely understanding.

Children inevitably ask themselves why their own parents are not like TV parents. Next to these ideal media figures, their own flesh-and-blood parents appear unfair and mean. It's difficult for parents to establish authority in the eyes of children who view them as inadequate in comparison to TV parents.

Television has also rendered most of *real* life uninteresting. Television programmers have learned to hold the interest of viewers by using technical changes. Scene changes, various camera angles, superimposition of multiple images, musical backgrounds, unique sound effects, and a host of other manipulations all work together to maintain the viewer's attention.

Television's ability to create an environment that is more interesting than real life makes it difficult for children to become involved in family activities. Attempts to get kids excited about family gatherings, trips, and other times of sharing are usually greeted by complaints from children who would rather watch television. Many parents have found that taking the family on a car trip through a national park turns out to be less than the happy "together time" they had planned. It's difficult for kids to get excited by the real Grand Canyon after they've experienced it from twenty different angles in less than fifteen seconds during a beer commercial. Constructing family activities that can compete with television techniques often proves to be a Herculean task for the average parent.

We youth leaders also have difficulties competing with television. It's difficult to maintain high interest in our Sunday-evening youth fellowship when TV has conditioned our kids to expect far more entertainment than the church can offer. We've heard endless tirades against the content of television programs, but we're now discovering that the *techniques* of programming are potentially far more dangerous.

Neil Postman, in his book *The Disappearance of Childhood*, has pointed out still another television-related problem. He claims that childhood must involve secrets that society keeps from the young. Society must shelter children from the cruelties and obscenities of adult existence.[4] Television, according to Postman, makes this kind of secrecy impossible. By the age of ten, the typical American young person has seen programs on incest, abortion, and homosexuality. The evening news has exposed kids to rapes, murders, wars, and more. Children who grow up watching TV know too much. They have no need to wait expectantly to learn the facts of life from their parents. Parenthood is thus denied one of its most important functions: introducing children to truths about the adult world. Because of TV, children already know these truths. As a result, Postman says, television has

75

brought childhood to an end, making parenting an ambiguous task at best.

ONE SOLUTION: AUTHORITARIANISM

Studies on cults and new religions show that often kids join these groups because membership delivers them from the tyranny of other-directedness. Young people find parent substitutes who authoritatively direct their lives and consequently deliver them from the uncertainties of *gesellschaft* life. It's no wonder that young people in these groups bow to every dictate of their leaders. They find it comforting at last to have "parents" who can give direction to their lives and spell out in detail what should be said and done each moment of every day.

Often, authoritarian youth groups can function much like cults. They too can deliver young people from the ambiguities of other-directed lives. When parents are afraid to dictate to their children, dictatorial youth leaders can become surrogate parents who direct the young people. Such symbiotic relationships are the basis of many youth programs.

There is a positive side to being in a youth group that spells out what is expected from Christian young people. I myself belonged to such a group and give it credit for my survival as a Christian. It was belonging to this group that made Romans 12:2 my favorite Bible verse ("Do not conform any longer to the pattern of this world, but be transformed by the renewing of your mind"). The guiding principle of our youth group was the verse "Come ye out from among them and be ye separate with the Lord" (2 Cor. 6:17). My youth group made it a heroic thing to reject other-direction and adopt a Christian lifestyle. I became obedient to my parents, submissive to their instruction, and respectful of their advice. I did what my parents expected of me, even if it went counter to the expectations of my secular high-school peers. I became inner-directed. Rather than caring primarily about what

others thought of me, I became committed ﹍
scriptural principles of how children should relate to ﹍
parents.

In contrast to all the criticisms that are leveled at Bill
Gothard and his seminars on *Basic Youth Conflicts*, many
parents defend his work with enthusiasm. These parents
point out that his ability to call young people to biblically
prescribed roles has made parenting much easier and more
enjoyable. While some may say that this potential blessing
comes at a high psychological price, the evidence seems to be
to the contrary. Studies indicate that the kind of obedience
Gothard's seminars produce is psychologically healthy.

A TOOL FOR MODERN TIMES:
THE DEMOCRATIC FAMILY

In his important book *Love and Conflict*, Christian
sociologist Gibson Winter contends that a good option for the
family facing the modern leadership crisis can be found in
what he calls "the democratic family." In this type of family
system, the parents are leaders but not dictators.[5] The
democratic family works when children are old enough to
enter into intelligent discussions and conferences on how
family activities should be conducted.

As my own children were growing up, we often called
family meetings in which conflicts and differences of opinion
were discussed. Sometimes the rules and regulations that
determined acceptable behavior were established. We even
decided together on what punishment would follow viola-
tions of the regulations. These discussions provided a good
opportunity for us as parents to communicate our values to
our children. The exchanges we had at these family meetings
gave us openings to show how we believed biblical principles
should be applied to the affairs of everyday life.

When my son began to drive, we had a long meeting to
establish fair expectations for using the car. We agreed that
certain forms of carelessness would not be allowed—and that

if they occurred, he would forfeit driving privileges for six months. One evening as I drove into our driveway, I found my son waiting for me. When I got out of my car, he handed me his set of car keys and his driver's license. I knew what had happened, and I appreciated his honesty. Discipline had been carried out without rancor. Democracy had proven to be a useful control system for the family.

In his book, Winter outlines a biblical case for the democratic family system. He contends that leadership for the Christian family was not meant to be authoritarian. His proposals for family decision making not only allow for the parental respect that God requires but also provide a realistic control system that is viable for modern urban living. In the democratic family, authoritarian dictates do not come from any one person but from the collective fellowship. The authority is in the group, so that members are responsible to each other and to themselves for what they do. The authority continues even when one or both parents are absent.

We in youth work would be wise to study and teach the democratic family model. At a time when parents are perplexed about how to control their children, this model can prove to be a brilliant alternative to the chaos that has become far too normative in American homes.

5 The Sexuality Wilderness

Recently I was asked if youth ministers had a theological agenda for the next decade. As I thought about the question, I realized how detached theology has become from the concerns of young people. Theology deals with metaphysics, eschatology, doctrine, and so on, but it seldom addresses young people's most pressing concern—their sexuality. As young people struggle to make their way through what Vance Packard has called "the Sexual Wilderness," there seems to be little biblically based theology to help them discern the meaning of their sexual lives and the "rightness" of their behavior.

Solving the puzzle of their sexuality is core to the psyche of all kids. Who they are, their sense of self-worth, their hopes for the future, even their spiritual destinies are inexorably linked to their sexual struggles. Every other issue and concern is dwarfed by the phenomenon of their sexuality.

CHANGING PATTERNS OF SEXUAL BEHAVIOR

Many people would claim that the sexual scene is basically the same today as it has always been. Young people have always been troubled by sexual temptations, have always found the restrictions of the adult community oppressive, and have always been preoccupied with sexual concerns. However, there *is* something that has changed dramatically—behavior.

79

The revolution in sexual behavior among American young people is astounding. While the church basically has maintained its traditional positions on sexual morality, the number of teenagers violating those norms has increased significantly. At the same time, young people have continued to remain religiously committed, creating within them a deep conflict. Their religious commitment condemns the behavior that has become increasingly normative for them. Consequently, their level of guilt along with the corresponding emotional problems has increased. It therefore isn't surprising to discover that suicide, depression, self-hatred, and despair have become epidemic within the youth culture.

It's difficult to get a clear picture of what's happening in the sexual lives of today's kids. They certainly are behaving in ways that are very different from young people in the 1950s. At the time of the famous Kinsey studies, approximately 14 percent of high-school girls and 25 percent of high-school boys had experienced sexual intercourse.[1] The general estimate for high-school teenagers in the 1980s is that 43 percent of the girls and 47 percent of the boys experience sexual intercourse before graduation.[2] It's interesting to note that the differential in statistics for girls in relationship to those for boys has significantly decreased, indicating the emergence of a new kind of sexual equality.

It's also interesting to note that while religious orientation influences young people's sexual behavior, it doesn't make the enormous difference youth ministers might expect. Studies show that of the church-related college students who considered themselves "very religious," 31 percent of the girls and 39 percent of the boys had had sexual intercourse by the time they graduated from high school.[3] Other statistics show that of the kids who hadn't had sexual intercourse during their high-school years, almost one-third fell into the category Alfred Kinsey and his associates euphemistically call "technical virgins." Although the "technical virgins" have not engaged in sexual intercourse, they have experienced petting that was intensive enough to stimulate orgasms.

STRUGGLING TO FIND BIBLICAL NORMS
HEAVY PETTING

Most youth ministers I know are able to make a case against premarital sexual intercourse. Using biblical texts related to fornication, they're able to support the traditional, religious position that condemns intercourse before marriage. However most youth ministers say very little about premarital petting and sexual activity that, were it followed by coitus, could be labeled as "intensive foreplay." Some references might be made to Galatians 5 and its descriptions of "the lusts of the flesh," but most youth ministers usually pass over the subject of heavy petting. It's an issue that is simply ignored. Yet "very religious" young people are statistically likely to engage in heavy petting.

MASTURBATION AND FANTASIZING

While many youth workers fail to discuss heavy petting, many will discuss the subject of masturbation. However, there seems to be no normative ethical position for these discussions. Some youth workers regard masturbation as God's blessing that allows young people to relieve their sexual tensions without violating his requisites for virginity before marriage. Others consider masturbation to be a sexual perversion that puts the practitioner in danger of eternal damnation. Most youth ministers simply accept the fact, without passing judgment on the practice, that kids masturbate.

Regardless of whether or not they view masturbation as acceptable behavior for their young people, most youth ministers have no idea how pervasive the practice is. Studies on premarital sexual behavior indicate that well over 90 percent of males and 78 percent of females masturbate.[4]

What discussions on masturbation often ignore altogether, however, is the role of fantasy in this activity. In actuality, fantasizing sexual intercourse while masturbating is almost a universal practice. With females, such fantasizing usually involves a person who is the object of love or infatuation. Males, however, are more likely to fantasize during masturbation about having intercourse with women whom they regard simply as sexual objects.

As you deal with the subject of masturbation, you should give some consideration to the fantasies that accompany the activity. Are such fantasies really fornication committed in the mind, and as such, are they just as condemnable as the act of fornication itself? Or are these fantasies harmless sublimations of sexual tensions that must be released if spiritual and emotional well-being is to be maintained?

A hypothetical example may prove helpful. John is an evangelical Christian. He isn't involved in heavy petting or sexual intercourse, but he does masturbate. When he does, he imagines that he's having sexual relations with Jane, a girl in his class. He doesn't date Jane and he's not even interested in a dating relationship with her. However, he finds her physically attractive and enjoys fantasizing about having sexual intercourse with her. He feels guilty about his behavior, and even though he's prayed for deliverance from the temptation to masturbate, he continues to do it. He's increasingly convinced that he's not a Christian because he believes that Christians have the spiritual strength to overcome the temptation to masturbate.

Several important questions are raised by John's dilemma. Is this fantasy sin? Is this fantasy an expression of a sexism that regards a female as a sexual object rather than a person? Is John a Christian? What should you say to John if John confesses this behavior to you?

HOMOSEXUALITY

Perhaps the area with which youth ministers are most apt to feel inadequate to deal is homosexual activity and orientation. The traditional Pauline explanation of the causes of homosexual behavior is taken from the first chapter of Romans. There the apostle Paul wrote of certain men and women who exhaust the gratifications of heterosexual activity and then degenerate into homosexual behavior as they seek new ways to satisfy their insatiable lusts.

It's interesting to note that some Christian homosexuals cite this very passage to justify their behavior and orientation. They point out that Paul is condemning heterosexual perverts. They claim their homosexual orientation is both natural and inborn.

However you happen to believe that the Christian faith would view homosexual orientation and behavior, you should be aware that such behavior isn't unusual. While as much as 9 percent of the male population and 5 percent of the female population are homosexual (that represents almost 14,000,000 Americans), studies from Kinsey's time up to present day indicate that as many as 43 percent of the male population and 20 percent of the female population have had serious homosexual experiences at some time during their lives.[5]

GUILT—OR LACK OF GUILT

Little research or theological reflection has been given to the emotional reactions of those who engage in sexual acts. Ira L. Reiss has provided some help along these lines.[6] His findings are, in some respects, surprising. He found that females were less likely than males to experience guilt after having premarital coitus. This, says Reiss, is probably due to the fact that females usually link sexual intercourse to a love relationship. The fact that the coital activity was with a loved person seemed to diminish guilt dramatically. Furthermore,

Reiss discovered that once a pattern of intense sexual relations is established, that pattern is seldom broken except through the termination of the relationship. In light of this, youth workers may want to advise couples who've become sexually involved to end their relationship temporarily, with the hope that by breaking the pattern of repetitious "illicit" behavior, a new and more wholesome relationship between the two persons may be established in the future.

Religious young people who are able to handle premarital coitus without guilt usually rationalize their behavior by saying, "We're going to get married anyway." Most claim that they're already married in the eyes of God and that they lack only society's recognition of their oneness.

Your responses to such assertions require that you develop a theology of marriage that provides some basis for making judgments about this matter. You must be able to answer many questions. When, according to Scripture, are people married? Is it when the ceremony takes place or when, as some claim, "the two become one flesh" (i.e. the act of sexual intercourse)?

ABORTION

The questions about abortion are too numerous and controversial to be discussed here. However, youth workers should note that somewhere around 11 percent of female teenagers have abortions. The reason this figure is not higher is because the social stigma associated with having children out of wedlock has disappeared, and unmarried women are choosing to keep their babies rather than putting them up for adoption or having abortions.

OUR CHALLENGE: PROVIDE ANSWERS

The theological questions related to sexuality beg for answers. Young people find the church's positions irrelevant or unrealistic as they struggle with issues related to their sexual identities. It's strange that in the face of such demands, many of us feel that the most pressing need is to come up with clever new ideas for our Sunday-evening fellowship hour or for our next social event. It's time for us to lead young people out of the sexual wilderness into a promised land where they will find real meaning and direction for their sexual lives.

One fruitful avenue to explore in defining a theology of sexuality is a biblically based perception of personhood. Instead of looking at biblical texts that either condemn or affirm sexual activities, it may be more useful to explore how the Bible instructs young people to view those persons with whom they become romantically involved. Strange as it may seem to those of us in the evangelical tradition, Martin Buber, a Jewish existentialist philosopher, may provide some important assistance in such a venture.[7]

Buber categorizes interpersonal relationships into two types. He believes that each person can have either an "I-It" relationship or an "I-Thou" relationship with another person. An "I-It" relationship is one in which the other person is treated as an object or a thing. The first person may look for rules that govern the actions that can be taken with regard to that "It." There even may be a rigid moral code controlling the interaction of the first person (the "I") with the other person (the "It"), but the other person still is viewed as an object.

In an "I-Thou" relationship, the other person is viewed as a *subject*. The first person tries to empathize with the other person, attempting to "enter into" the other person emotionally, to experience reality from the other person's subjective stance. The "I-Thou" relationship, as Buber describes it, is an even deeper relationship than those described by humanistic psychologists. Buber contends that in the "I-Thou" relationship, the first person senses in the encounter an experience of a transcendental dimension in the personhood of the other. God is experienced! God is encountered! This way of relating to another person, says Buber, surprises a

85

person with the awareness that he or she is relating not only to a temporal human being but also to that which is eternal, divine, and infinite.

Buber makes no apology for the obvious mystical quality of the "I-Thou" relationship that he attempts to describe and believes it is beyond verbal expression. He boldly claims that in every human encounter lies the possibility for the discerning spiritual person to encounter God. Behind every temporal, human "Thou," says Buber, waits the "Eternal Thou."

Buber's interpretation of what can potentially be encountered in the other person is paralleled and supported by biblical revelation. In Matthew 25, Jesus invites each of us to recognize that he is personally waiting to be encountered in the persons we meet in our day-to-day experiences. When Jesus declared "whatever you did for one of the least of these brothers of mine, you did for me" (Matt. 25:40), he laid a basis for acknowledging that the sacred Presence is waiting for discovery in our relationships with others.

Other biblical passages also suggest that every human encounter holds the potentiality for divine encounter. Passages such as John 1:4 ("In him was life, and that life was the light of men") and passages in which we are referred to as temples in which God dwells (see Acts 7:48; 17:28; 1 Cor. 6:19; 2 Cor. 6:16) richly support the affirmation that the presence of Jesus is waiting to be met in the other.

Such a theology of personhood has tremendous implications for sexual interaction. If the "other person" in a romantic relationship is viewed as a mystical incarnation of God, then the two people will respect what they say and do to each other. Exploitation of the other person for the purpose of sexual gratification will be out of the question. Instead, the two people will try to lift up and enhance each other in all they do. Anything that would cheapen or diminish the dignity and worth of the other will be shunned.

Sexual interaction suddenly possesses a sacred dimension that prescribes how persons should relate to each other.

Too often, the "other person" has been treated as an "It." One can use a thing, exploit an object, and manipulate an "It" for one's own satisfaction. When the other person is recognized as a temple of the "Eternal Thou," however, everything changes. The exploration of these changes provides a solid basis for the relevant theology you'll need to develop to bring the power of the Christian view of sexuality and sexual behavior into your young people's hearts and lives.

PART 2

SOCIOLOGICAL CONSIDERATIONS IN YOUTH-MINISTRY PROGRAMMING

6 What Color Is Your Evangelism? Your Outreach Program

Almost every Christian group agrees that outreach is a vitally important part of its life. The survival of *any* group over an extended period of time is dependent on taking in new members, but Christian groups believe they have a divine imperative to do more than survive. They believe they're called to change the world.

However, Christian groups disagree about *how* outreach should be done. Some emphasize being "saved" and entering into a personal relationship with Jesus. Others downplay efforts to solicit converts and focus outreach on working for social justice—which, they feel, gives evidence that the kingdom of God is manifesting itself in history. Some Christians try to reach out to the world through tracts, radio broadcasts, and street meetings, while others witness "by example."

Debate over styles and objectives of outreach can be intense, at times resulting in name calling and schisms. Many Christian groups have developed theologies to legitimate various styles of outreach, and to them, these theologies can become as sacred as the gospel message itself.

THE INFLUENCE OF SOCIOECONOMIC STATUS ON EVANGELISTIC STYLE

What many Christians fail to recognize is that socioeconomic factors often influence styles of evangelism more than either the Bible or the Holy Spirit. In his book *The Social*

Sources of Denominationalism, H. Richard Niebuhr, a prominent sociologist and theologian of a generation ago, identified a variety of these factors and demonstrated how they condition the forms and styles of outreach and evangelism throughout Christendom.[1] Niebuhr showed that of all the sociological influences on outreach styles, none had a more significant influence than the socioeconomic status of group members. He found that the class identity of a given group determined, more than anything else, how that group would relate to the society in which it was set.

Using a typology borrowed from the German sociologist Ernst Troeltsch, Niebuhr suggested that the religious style of the lower socioeconomic classes could be identified as *sectarian,* while the religious style of the middle to upper classes could be labeled *ecclesiastic.* (In America, ecclesiastic religion is usually associated with mainstream denominationalism.) According to Niebuhr, these two religious types are found at opposite ends of a continuum. Each has a specific, socially prescribed world view that expresses itself in a specific and distinctive style of evangelism.

The distinctive world views of sectarian and ecclesiastic Christians, drawn from their respective socioeconomic environments, radically affect how each group views the society they are attempting to influence for Christ. Those world views particularly affect how each group believes the converts should live out their faith in the world.

SECTARIAN EVANGELISM:
BROTHER, ARE YOU SAVED?

Members of sectarian groups are generally drawn from what Niebuhr called the "socially disinherited" parts of the population. Sectarians tend to come from the less prestigious areas of their respective communities. They often dominate the lower-paying jobs and are, for the most part, less educated than those who align with more ecclesiastical religious groups.

Growing up with a sense of social disinheritance can generate a counterreaction against society. Sectarians tend to put down the society they feel has rejected them. Sectarian youth groups often express their rejection of the world by establishing a pietistic lifestyle they label "holy." They contrast their lifestyle with what they consider to be the "worldly" lifestyle typical of middle-class Americans.

This pietistic sectarian lifestyle is easy to identify. It manifests itself in a rejection of rock music, smoking, drinking, dancing, and other behavior considered evil—even demonically inspired—and designed to stimulate the "lusts of the flesh." The language of the sectarian youth group differs from that of the world; a special religious vocabulary comes into play—romantic dates are "times of fellowship" and decisions are "leadings of the Lord."

The evangelistic task of sectarian youth leaders is never complete until their young people are socialized into this mindset. They must direct their converts away from what they consider to be humanistic thought and behavior and toward "the truth." The leaders' efforts are culminated when their youth-group members who go on to higher education attend Bible schools or colleges that espouse their separatist lifestyle.

The style of evangelistic outreach generated by this world view encourages individual decisions that result in personal conversion to the Christian faith. Sectarians will use any ethical means available to promote the truths they see as the core of the gospel message. Sectarian outreach often includes, for example, tract distribution and neon signs that declare to a lost world that "Jesus saves." Sectarians believe that "faith comes from hearing the message, and the message is heard through the word of Christ" (Rom. 10:17).

Many television and radio evangelists (Robert Schuller being a notable exception) appeal to the sectarian mindset. They espouse a religious philosophy that views personal conversion as the cure for most, if not all, of society's woes.

Their promotion of the gospel through methods which, to their critics, seem to parallel the marketing practices of those selling toothpaste and deodorant is often an embarrassment to those outside the sectarian perspective.

Sectarians have an urgency about their outreach efforts, built on the assumption that their way of salvation is the only way. Sectarians are haunted by their belief that every day thousands of people die and go to hell because they didn't believe in Jesus. The love and concern sectarians feel for the lost drives them to use all methods available to save people from a Christless eternity. They admit that grabbing "sinners" by their coat labels and asking, "Buddy, are you saved?" might be a bit aggressive, but they claim that at least it shows they care.

ECCLESIASTIC EVANGELISM: LET'S CHANGE THE WORLD TOGETHER

Ecclesiastic youth leaders, on the other hand, project a more accommodating attitude toward the dominant culture. They are eager to prove that they can be "cool" in the eyes of typical teenagers. They promote the idea that a Christian lifestyle can be culturally normal.

Ecclesiastic youth groups seek to socialize their members into the dominant values of the culture. They operate on the assumption that American society was designed to be just; people experience discrimination and oppression when the social system doesn't function as it was designed to do.

Those who develop the ideologies and programs for these youth groups contend that central to Christian youth ministry is the challenge to improve the social order so that the ideals of America (which are viewed as being synonymous with the principles of justice cited in the Scriptures) might be realized. Peter Berger, one of the leaders in the field of sociology of religion, contends that ecclesiastic Christians view the world as OK and define the task of the church as improving a basically good world so that the inadequacies that do exist in the American social system can be over-come.[2]

Ecclesiastic youth groups tend to reject the zealous style of personal evangelism that characterizes most sectarian youth groups. Ecclesiastic youth groups often are full of people who are members because they were "born into the church" rather than because they were "born again." Those who grow up in a religious tradition seldom exhibit the zeal that is common among those who experience the "first love" (Rev. 2:4) of the religious experience so characteristic of new converts. Some people believe that young people raised in an ecclesiastic youth group may be inoculated with pseudo-christianity and are therefore immune to the real "disease."

The ecclesiastic group's motivation to evangelize is fueled by the belief that religious people can live richer, fuller lives in our OK world. They believe that religious faith facilitates the integration of young people into prominent social positions that will allow them to contribute to the well-being of others. Outreach, then, includes all attempts to help young people experience everything life has to offer. And the "good news" is that God is establishing his kingdom and is liberating oppressed peoples, like minorities and women.

Will Herberg, whose brilliant book *Protestant, Catholic, Jew* still stands as a seminal work in the study of cultural religion, argues that the religion of the American middle class tends to affirm each of the three dominant American religions as being of equal value.[3] Ecclesiastic Christians, according to Herberg, claim that those who believe Christians are the only viable candidates for heaven are narrow and bigoted. When Bailey Smith, the one-time president of the Southern Baptist Convention, announced that God hears the prayers only of Christians, the public outcry in ecclesiastic circles was intense.

According to Herberg, faith in faith, rather than faith in Jesus, is the basis for salvation among the mainline American religionists. Consequently the drive to convert the lost to

95

Christ, so typical of sectarians, is played down in ecclesiastic youth groups. Evangelistic crusades are not their specialty. They are, in fact, often repulsed by sectarian evangelistic methods. They opt for outreach strategies aimed at what they believe to be the less-arrogant goal of improving the social order.

Ecclesiastic Christians justify their ideological emphases from a theological framework that contends that the gospel is the declaration of a new socioeconomic order inherent in the biblical concept of *jubilee*. They believe that the kingdom of God is to be established in this world rather than the next. Ecclesiastic outreach includes all words and deeds that encourage the process whereby God's kingdom comes to be manifested on earth as it is in heaven.

These distinctives between sectarian and ecclesiastic world view and evangelistic styles are by no means exclusive. Many sectarians demonstrate social consciousness; many ecclesiastic Christians recognize the importance of personal evangelism. What these emphases illustrate is that each group has a different primary purpose for outreach. Sectarians work to get people saved for heaven, while ecclesiastic Christians focus on transforming the world into a social system that conforms to biblical requisites for justice.

BURN THOSE BRIDGES

Gerlach and Hine, in their book *People, Power and Change,* noted that religious groups requiring high levels of commitment from their members require "bridge-burning" acts.[4] These acts separate new recruits from their former friends and give newcomers a sense of belonging to their new religious group. Outreach efforts can serve as such "bridge-burning" acts for Christian youth groups. Interestingly, both sectarian and ecclesiastic youth leaders seek, and attain, identical "bridge-burning" experiences for their young people, although they would see their methods as quite different.

I was a product of the evangelistic efforts of a sectarian church. Shortly after my teenage conversion, the other members of my youth group let me know that evangelizing my friends at school would be the true test of my faith. If I were really alive in Christ, I was told, I would witness to my classmates. Using analogies from biology, they pointed out that all life reproduces itself; any caring Christian should seek to reproduce his or her new life in others. Such arguments played no small role in motivating me to become a bold propagator of the gospel at West Philadelphia High School.

My evangelistic efforts did exactly what Gerlach and Hine said is essential to establishing firm membership in the community of Christians. Most of my friends were turned off by my preaching, and they rejected me. My youth group congratulated me for being "persecuted for righteousness' sake," claiming that this is what happens to all true servants of God. A "we/they" dichotomy was established, and I was irrevocably established in the "we" group of Christians who were set against the "they" group who were "of the world." I have no evidence that my outreach effort converted any of my former friends, but it no doubt carried me into a new and higher level of commitment to the Christian group.

Gerlach and Hine contended that participation in a public demonstration for social justice also can effect the kind of psychological transformation so essential for membership in high-commitment groups. Marches on Washington and Ban-the-Bomb rallies seldom convince politicians to change policies, but such demonstrations do change those who participate in them. The anti-war activities of the 1960s solidified thousands of young people into a movement whose members had a deep commitment to one another. The marches on state capitols led by Martin Luther King turned unorganized, discontented blacks into a unified political movement that changed the course of history.

TAKING THE BEST FROM BOTH

What lessons can we learn from our observation of the two religious styles that dominate our culture? And more important, how shall we approach outreach in our own ministries? God uses both sectarian and ecclesiastic Christians to accomplish his purposes, regardless of the weaknesses inherent in each style. Yet we may vastly strengthen both the effectiveness and maturity of our own outreach efforts when we synthesize what is strong from both traditions and establish a more holistic approach to evangelism. No matter what background we come from, we can see that there is much to respect, and imitate, in that "other" tradition that may seem so foreign to us.

For example, many—if not most—ecclesiastic Christians who put down the aggressive evangelistic style of sectarian religion admit that they themselves became dedicated Christians through affiliating with the very kind of sectarian programs they now condemn. While speaking at a mainline denominational seminary recently, I asked my audience how many of them had become Christians through sectarian-type evangelistic programs. More than two-thirds of those present raised their hands. Though some of us may be uncomfortable with what we see as "simplistic" evangelism, without such efforts, many of us wouldn't be where we are today.

Sectarians also can raise questions for all of us about our response to the truly worldly lifestyle of contemporary youth culture. Red flags should be run up to caution young people about the unchristian practices and values encouraged by rock music. In addition, though smoking and drinking aren't necessarily signs of being hell-bound, they *are* destructive habits. Smoking can cause cancer; alcohol is a potentially deadly, addictive drug that is currently wreaking havoc among teenagers.

On the other hand, sectarians must recognize that

"getting saved" is more than getting ready for the next life. Salvation should be viewed as enlistment in a movement committed to transforming this world into the kind of world God wills for it to be. God loves this world and wants to make it into his kingdom. He wants all "principalities and powers" transformed into social structures that will serve his purposes and be a blessing to all humanity. Conversion should be seen as a process through which young people can become God's agents of change in this world.

Such a view of what Christians should seek to accomplish through their outreach programs doesn't require the naïve optimism that characterized some of the "social-gospel" thinking of the early part of this century. It's not true that people of goodwill can create a just world without God's intervention in history. But God saves us by his grace in order to initiate through us the creation of his kingdom, which he will establish in its fullness at the end of the age. We can help our kids see that God has saved them from sin so that they can become heroic disciples whose destiny is to do God's work in the world.

My own particular perspective on the biblical concept of the kingdom of God leads me to suggest that converts to Christ should become persons who are committed to far more than the improvement of a basically good America. God is calling into being a group of radical young people committed to the transformation of the current social order. Futurologists argue that the normative American lifestyle requires the consumption of unrenewable mineral resources at a rate that will exhaust them within a century. The polluting of our environment threatens life on this planet, and we have created an economic system that thrives on military spending and requires that we support oppressive political regimes to maintain its stability.

These evils—and they *are* evils—must be challenged and ended. For this to happen, young people must be converted to Christ and become his agents for a nonviolent revolution that will challenge the present order of things and struggle for the realization of God's kingdom within history. This kind of outreach requires zealous, Spirit-filled converts committed to a vision of the world inspired by the biblical revelation. When our outreach programs generate such converts, the dichotomy between personalistic salvation and social conversion will disappear. We will see a powerful linking of the evangelistic imperatives of sectarian Christians and the social concerns of ecclesiastic believers—the holistic outreach strategy that has been God's wonderful plan from the beginning.

7 Counseling:
The Inescapable Privilege

Counseling has always been part of youth workers' job descriptions. In the old days when evangelicals used youth rallies primarily as a means to proselytize, counseling was an essential part of the youth worker's job. Following the invitation to come down the aisle and publicly declare faith in Christ, young people were counseled in the back room, while their friends waited on the buses that would take them home. In such after-meeting counseling sessions, youth workers helped teenagers to clarify the decisions they had just made. It's my belief that a survey would show that most of the young people who made commitments to Christ at such rallies and stayed in the faith did so, not so much as a consequence of a great sermon, but as the result of the efforts of those who were willing to take the time to give them personal counseling.

Today's youth worker has been influenced by the emergence of relational theologies—theologies that suggest that young people experience the love of Christ through meaningful personal relationships. Relational theologians claim that Christ's love incarnated in the youth worker's personal encounters with teenagers is more likely to result in meaningful salvation experiences than are attempts to lead kids to Christ through mass meetings. Some of the more mystical relational theologians apply Buber's "I-Thou" model and claim that we experience the dynamic presence of the Holy Spirit through in-depth relationships. Whatever the value of these relational theologies, they've made counseling a crucial instrument in youth ministry.

OPENING PANDORA'S BOX

When Sigmund Freud initiated psychoanalysis, he seriously wondered whether his clients would reveal to him the deep, dark secrets of their lives. Much to his surprise, he learned that his clients were desperate to share their private lives, eager to unload the painful psychological baggage they had carried for a lifetime. He said that pent-up stories of private sufferings seemed to ooze from their every pore.[1]

Youth workers today find a similar experience. They find themselves deeply involved with the sociopsychological problems of the teenagers they counsel. Listening to young people in personal counseling situations can open Pandora's box. Youth workers frequently discover that what they thought would be nothing more than a simple presentation of the Four Spiritual Laws ends up in a discussion of deep-seated social and psychological maladjustments. Often without realizing what they are getting into, youth workers find themselves in sessions that require them to function as much like amateur psychologists as messengers of God's Word.

THE SECRET LIFE OF KIDS

As youth workers become friends with the kids they serve, they hear startling things. Recent studies have revealed that nearly 15 percent of all children have been sexually molested and that 20 percent of all teenage females have had to endure rapes.[2] Such trauma can lead to severe psychological maladjustments that can surface quickly in the context of a loving conversation.

I recall listening to a thirteen-year-old girl after a talk I had given. She told me she was too sinful to become a Christian. When I asked why she felt that way, she admitted that her father had sexually molested her when she was ten years old. Like most little girls at that age, she had a sexual attraction for her father, and when her father exploited that interest, she "liked how it felt." From this she concluded that she must be a bad person. Because she wanted to love her father, she assumed that she was the one who was responsible for what had happened between them. I urged her to see a licensed psychotherapist, but she refused because she didn't want to get her father into trouble. She claimed that she told me what had happened only because she trusted me and knew that I'd never tell anyone else. Whether or not I wanted to be, I was her only counselor. With whatever limited knowledge and skill I had at my disposal, I was the sole partner in her dark secret. Furthermore, I knew that she probably wouldn't enter into any kind of positive relationship with Christ if I couldn't help her work through her painful problem. Such situations are common for all of those who work with young people for any extended period of time.

LEARNING TO SAY NO

Like it or not, youth workers are forced to listen to painful descriptions of the things young people are desperate to reveal. Youth workers who are readily available find themselves inundated with teenagers anxious to unburden themselves of problems too heavy for them to handle alone. The pressures that come from being an available counselor may be more than the average youth worker can handle.

A young seminary graduate I know went to serve as the youth pastor of a large church in an affluent, Midwestern suburb. He was an engaging young man whose empathetic manner gave him instant rapport with his youth group. His youth fellowship group grew rapidly. Teenagers flocked to his church as word spread that this new youth pastor was available to listen to their problems. Soon, almost every available minute in his life was consumed by counseling. Young people were constantly in his office. His home became a teenage hangout where soulful discussions regularly went on into the late hours of the night. Burdened with a messianic complex, this young pastor lacked the will or the desire to turn away anyone who needed help. Regardless of how exhausted he became or how inconvenient the time, he was always ready to counsel his kids. His new wife began to resent the time she had to give up so that her husband could counsel young people. Whenever she begged for time, her husband made her feel guilty for being so selfish as to put her wants above the spiritual needs of those seeking his counsel.

Their marriage eventually was ruined. The youth pastor, turned off by the sullenness of his resentful wife, became sexually involved with an eighteen-year-old girl from his youth group. The lives of several people were ruined because this young pastor couldn't set limits on his availability. Cases like this are not unusual. Youth workers, especially those who feel driven by some theological imperative to meet the needs of every teenager, are soon burned out and become vulnerable to self-destruction.

THE DEPENDENCY SYNDROME
Youth workers must be aware that those who need counseling often appear to be unable to survive without constant attention. Youth workers may find that one or two young people can fill up their entire work week. This may be ego gratifying, but it usually results in very sick relationships. Dependent teenagers often fall in love with their youth workers and can become quite sexually seductive in pursuing an ongoing relationship. Youth workers, particularly those who have inordinate needs for self-importance, have a hard time resisting such adoration. And the results can be disastrous.

ARE YOUTH WORKERS QUALIFIED TO BE COUNSELORS?
Some counseling professionals argue that counseling is too dangerous to be left in the hands of amateur youth workers. These critics claim that youth workers who don't

have the insights and the professional skills of trained, certified counselors shouldn't be messing in the complex lives of young people. They feel that amateurs can do more harm than good.

On the other hand, many people (and I include myself) are not convinced that good counseling is the result of using some complicated, scientific techniques. Some of us argue that counseling is a gift, given to some and not to others. Max Weber, one of the founding fathers of sociology, calls the gift *verstehen*.[3] Charles Cooley, the famous American social psychologist, calls it *sympathetic introspection*.[4] Others believe that counseling is an art form rather than a science and that the good counselor is one who has a God-given ability to enter empathically into the subjective consciousness of another person and to perceive reality from that other person's perspective.

Those of us who hold these positions sometimes question whether sociology and psychology are really as scientific as many of their proponents claim them to be.[5] While we respect social science's contribution toward the healing of persons, we also believe that the ability to gain insight into another person's psyche is dependent more on possessing a mystical gift of the Spirit than on having the proper academic training. We believe that a youth worker with the gift is a better counselor than a professionally trained psychotherapist without the gift. We believe that the academic mystique that disparages the amateur is sometimes an unnecessary example of intellectual arrogance.[6]

Both arguments are true to some extent. There are dangers to both counselor and counselee any time one human being tries to help another at a significant psychospiritual level. What we in youth work must do is to understand both our counseling potential and our counseling limits. We must try to gain as much knowledge and help from the professional therapeutic field as we possibly can; we must learn to discern what types of situations and problems are outside the limits of our abilities and need to be referred to trained, licensed professionals.

WHEN, AND TO WHOM, SHOULD WE REFER?

But how do we know when we should refer someone? And to whom will we refer the person? Here are three general guidelines:

1. *Refer people who are dangerous to themselves or to others.* First, youth workers should know the warning signs of suicide and should get help for a person who may kill herself or himself. Second, youth workers should be able to recognize the symptoms of sociopaths who pose violent threats to the people around them.

2. *Learn the differences between psychoanalysis, psychotherapy, and psychiatry.* A knowledge of who can do what is crucial if we are to make truly helpful referrals. It's also important to be able to determine what type of help is needed. We could mistakenly assume, for example, that the ongoing depression of a particular teenager is due to psychological causes, when, in reality, the depression may be biophysically based. If we know enough to figure out that the latter is the case, a referral could be made to a psychiatrist, who would be able to prescribe the necessary medication. Authoritative text-books on abnormal psychology and counseling seminars can help youth workers become familiar with these early screening techniques.

3. *Learn about the different models for counseling—and the different views of the self—prescribed by the various counseling traditions.* If referrals are necessary, we should be able to direct troubled teenagers to professional counselors who have views of personhood that are in harmony with the Christian orientation that we ourselves espouse.

The concept of the nature of the self held by a therapist determines how that therapist will work with a client. Many young people have been messed up because well-meaning pastors and youth workers have referred them to therapists whose understanding of human nature was at odds with the Christian faith. A youth pastor in Denver once referred a troubled teenage girl to an agnostic psychoanalyst whose personal Freudian perspective on human nature was anti-Christian. In the course of counseling, the analyst suggested to this teenager that the source of her problems was an overdeveloped superego built on her deep religious beliefs. The analyst counseled this girl to reject her biblically based negative judgments about premarital sex. The girl followed his advice, but instead of becoming psychologically healthier, she became sexually promiscuous and, consequently, pathologically depressed. It was several years before this young woman would have anything to do with the church. It was only after she was referred to a Christian counselor who was able to help her work through most of her problems from a Christian perspective that she was able to find release from her deep feelings of guilt and to live a relatively happy life.

Youth workers will find sound direction and help in Rich Van Pelt's *Intensive Care: Helping Teenagers in Crisis* (Zondervan/Youth Specialties). The book includes a helpful chapter about crisis intervention as well as one about when and how to refer someone.

RECOGNIZING OUR STRENGTHS

What is our potential as counselors? If we have a firm grasp of how the Bible relates to personal problems, we can assist troubled kids to discover how God wants them to change. The emphasis on nondirective techniques, so strongly advocated by psychotherapists like Carl Rogers, has generated an unwarranted hesitancy for youth workers to spell out the biblical prescriptions for life's difficulties.[7] Too often, we forget that our first responsibility is to counsel young people according to the Bible.

As a student of the major philosophers and social scientists of modern times, I'm amazed at how often the most profound insights of such intellectual giants have been anticipated in the Scriptures.[8] Consequently, I'm surprised by the fact that so many youth workers counsel as if they're ashamed of the gospel of Christ. They tend to shy away from being direct in their counseling, even though directness is often just what their kids want. When young people go to church leaders for counsel, it's partly because they really want to learn what God has to say about their problems. In recent years, leading psychologists like William Glasser have reintroduced directive techniques that affirm to us that counselors sometimes can say, "Thus saith the Lord!"[9] Jay Adams, professor of practical theology at Westminster Theological Seminary, has been trying to communicate that truth to the religious community for decades, but it's only recently that we have begun to understand the importance of his claims.[10]

WHAT ABOUT US?

Freud believed that those who would be psychoanalysts must themselves go through psychoanalysis. He believed that it's important for those of us who deal with other people's problems to be persons who understand our own problems. Otherwise, we may end up imposing our own problems on those who come to us for counsel. He further taught that only those who subjectively understand what it's like to be counseled are in a position from which to counsel others effectively.

What Freud prescribed for psychoanalysts is worthwhile advice for all of us. We will be less effective than we could be in our work with young people if we resist our own need for regular counseling. As a young Baptist pastor, I sought counseling from the rector of an Episcopal church. (I had a special problem that he felt was beyond his ability to handle and so referred me to a Christian psychotherapist.) I sought counseling outside my denomination because I was afraid that giving in-depth knowledge of my flaws and shortcomings to someone in the Baptist church might come back to haunt me and mar my professional career. My fears were in part a product of my own insecurities about needing counseling at all, but too often, leaders are not expected to have (or allowed to admit to any) problems. For many reasons, most people involved in the helping professions are remarkably resistant to seeking help for themselves, and youth ministers are no exception. But whether we seek help within our own denominations or outside them, we must be open to receiving help that we need before we are ready to reach out to our young people.

THE INESCAPABLE PRIVILEGE

Counseling is an inescapable part of youth ministry. Those of us who have chosen this vocation must be willing to study to show ourselves approved unto God, becoming youth workers who need not be ashamed: rightly dividing the Word of Truth, keeping abreast of available training and resources, guarding against the tendency toward a messiah complex, and willing to submit ourselves to counseling. Given the pressing needs of our young people, these steps are necessary; given the tremendous opportunity we have as youth ministers to be an agent of God's healing Spirit, these steps are more than worth their personal cost to us.

8 Crisis Counseling: Praxis

Joan visits Haiti and confronts the suffering of children in that Third World nation. As she looks into the eyes of these desperate children, she is mystically aware that Christ is present in them. She remembers the verse of Scripture: "whatever you did for one of the least of these brothers of mine, you did for me" (Matt. 25:40). Joan is convinced that to be a Christian requires commitment to Third World peoples, and she becomes as missionary.

John is having sexual relations regularly with his fiancée. He believes that such behavior is contradictory to what is taught in Scripture, and he feels deep guilt. John goes to talk with his youth minister, who instructs him to make a decision—to choose between being a Christian or continuing his sexual involvement with his fiancée. John decides to give up his sexual involvement and obey what he believes Scripture teaches. From that day on, John believes the Bible to be inerrant, and his commitment to Christ follows a highly evangelical pattern.

The two stories I've just sketched are quite different, but they have one element in common: they each illustrate the principle of *praxis*—a principle that is changing the way people think about counseling and behavioral therapy. I feel that praxis has great significance for youth workers who want to influence their young people's attitudes and behavior for the sake of the gospel.

WHAT IS PRAXIS?

Praxis is a new word to many of us. *Webster's New World Dictionary* defines praxis as "practice, as distinguished from theory, of an art, science, etc." Put another way, praxis is a process through which a person creates a philosophy of life and an explanation of why things are as they are. Praxis is a personal struggle through which that person constructs an interpretation of the social and spiritual events that have impacted his or her life.

Because the principle of praxis is gaining increasing notice and favor among social scientists, some observers might suspect praxis to be just another form of relativism or Freudian rationalization. It isn't. What praxis means is that the person *feels* what the truth ought to be but hasn't yet developed an intellectual belief system or ideology to support his or her felt convictions.

Praxis does have a certain affinity to existentialist philosophy in that it moves toward a nonrationalistic basis for truth. Those who promote the concept of praxis contend that truth is beyond rationality and that rational belief systems are established to support convictions already deduced from experience.

Blaise Pascal (the seventeenth-century French Christian who gave us both calculus and modern existentialism) once said, "The heart has reasons that reason can never know." He was suggesting that once the heart establishes what is true, rational processes are employed to give "truth justifications" that make sense within the existing sociocultural system.[1] Unlike rationalization, which tries to make what is wrong right, praxis tries to help a person who has discovered what is right through nonrationalistic means establish a rational justification for what he or she has come to believe.

WHAT MAKES PRAXIS DIFFERENT?

What makes praxis different from other styles of constructing a belief system for life is its nonrationalistic character. The Greek philosophers taught that the way people *think* determines how they will *act;* advocates of praxis contend the opposite.

Those who advocate praxis believe that what a person *does* determines what a person *thinks.* In short, action determines ideology; action determines what one believes to be real; action determines religious convictions.

Take Joan's case, for instance. Through her *action*—visiting Haiti—her ideology was reshaped. Her rationalistic presuppositions about God and his imperatives for her life were altered when she came face-to-face with the empiric reality of human suffering. Jesus' statements in Matthew 25 became compelling after her nonrational Third World experience.

SHOULD WE REJECT PRAXIS?

Praxis has been promoted by Marxist philosophers. As Marxist thought has filled the vacuum created by the demise of alternative ideologies within Western academic circles, the concept has gained popularity. We can expect to come across the praxis concept more and more as we read the works of learning theorists and educational philosophists. Furthermore, the growing popularity of the Marxist-based "Liberation Theology" has given significant impetus to the propagation of the praxis concept in Christian discussions.

The fact that the idea is Marxist based is enough for some Christians to reject it. However, I believe that truth is truth, regardless of who articulates it. We must judge concepts in terms of their validity rather than by their promoters. If praxis accurately describes the way people develop their belief systems, then youth workers can't afford the luxury of discounting it simply because of its origins and primary promoters.

If a Christian is someone who believes in Jesus, then according to the praxis principle, *doing* the things Jesus would do makes a person a believer. Religious beliefs are constructed not through intellectual arguments based on rationalistic deductions but through actions.

The praxis principle suggests that the "doers of the word" are the only ones who become believers in the Word (see James 1). It suggests that obedience to God's will makes people into intellectually convinced Christians. Vice versa, disobedience to God's will makes people into skeptics.

Pascal suggested the praxis principle long ago when he stated that "atheism was born in disobedience."[2] According to Pascal, a person who disobeys what he or she believes to be God's will experiences an inner tension that creates anxiety and depression. The person senses guilt over his or her action. If the guilt is severe enough, he or she will be driven to take action to alleviate this inner pain and self-condemnation. The person either will repent of the disobedient activity and affirm with renewed vigor a commitment to God or reject his or her belief in God and no longer feel judged for the action that gave rise to this inner tension. If a person loves or enjoys a sin enough, he or she will reject God. Thus, atheism is the result of sinful action rather than sinful action being the result of atheism.

AN EXAMPLE OF PRAXIS IN THE OLD TESTAMENT

According to Søren Kierkegaard, Abraham obeyed God when he took Isaac to the mountain and offered him as a sacrifice to the Lord (Gen. 22:1–18). Afterward, a theology was constructed to set this act of absolute obedience in a meaningful context.[3] If Abraham had allowed his *a priori* theology—what he knew about God at that time—to direct his actions, he wouldn't have obeyed him.

Hebrews 6:13–20 gives us the meaning of Abraham's action in retrospect. Before the act and its subsequent consequences, Abraham's actions would not have been justified within his existing theology and cosmology. The story of Abraham and Isaac is a classic demonstration of the praxis principle.

That some people use the Kierkegaardian interpretation of the Abraham story to justify situational ethics is evidence to me of how easy it is to misconstrue both the Bible and Kierkegaard's theological suspension of ethics. What is being said, by both the Bible and Kierkegaard, is that Abraham *obeyed* God in a radical and unquestioning manner and didn't allow the limitations of his knowledge about God to provide a host of reasons why another course of action would've been more "moral."

If Abraham had been guided by situational ethics, he wouldn't have done what he did. *Praxis makes obedience to God more important than theologies about God.*

PRAXIS IN CRISIS COUNSELING

If the praxis principle is valid, then a crisis in a young person's life holds the best opportunity for character formation. Furthermore, the *way* the youth worker tries to help the person in crisis will be contingent on the praxis principle.

The teenager in crisis is creating a life theology and a philosophy that will wipe away many of the propositional faith statements that have been drilled into his or her head through years of social conditioning and religious education. What the teenager *does* to get out of the crisis may determine his or her thinking about God and everything else.

If the action that provides deliverance is best explained in the context of a world view in which Jesus is Lord, then the person will believe that Jesus is Lord. On the other hand, if the resolution of the crisis makes sense or is justifiable only within a world view in which there is no God, then an atheistic belief will emerge from the crisis. The youth worker, consequently, should concentrate on suggesting courses of action that will be congruent with a Christian commitment. If praxis is true—if what a teenager does will influence what that teenager thinks—then *more important than directing the young person's thinking is directing the young person's action.*

This assumption and its implications for counseling strategy take on clarity as we turn our attention back to John's situation. Rather than embarking on a painstaking examination of John's belief system and comparing it with

115

orthodox Christian teaching, his minister pointed John in the direction of behavioral change. When the behavioral decision had been made and implemented, the minister could then supply John with the theological and ideological rationale for his decision.

We shouldn't conclude that praxis rejects a rational thinking process. Quite the opposite. The praxis principle *requires* extensive rational activity. What praxis acknowledges is the *place* of thinking. The building of a rational system, be it a philosophy or a theology, is created after action. Theology is an ideology created in the process of being obedient to God.

DOES PRAXIS HAVE DANGERS?

Anyone who has read this far might give some credence to the praxis principle but might quickly add, "there must be balance." I agree! While I believe that we construct theologies by the ways in which we work through life's crises, I also contend that our beliefs establish our options for action.

Robert Merton, one of the deans of modern sociology, suggests that we adopt a "serendipity pattern of investigation."[4] By that, he means that our actions are always informed by what we think, but the unexpected and unintended consequences of what we do force us to recast our thoughts. According to Merton, thought provides options for action in times of crisis, but the choice of action taken by a person in crisis will force that person to redefine what is a plausible belief system. I think Merton is right.

In other words: If a *Christian* teenager comes for counseling in a time of crisis, the youth worker should be prepared to show that teenager the courses of action prescribed by Scripture (because the teenager probably holds a fairly high view of the authority of Scripture). As the young person obeys the biblically prescribed course of action, the youth worker should then help him or her construct a theology that puts the action, and its consequences, in a system that provides plausibility and faith. Crisis situations, then, become opportunities for creating faith and establishing theologies for life. This is clearly what happened in John's story.

Jay Adams and others whose counseling philosophies advocate directing people to act on biblical principles will find support in the implications of praxis. Ironically, a Marxist insight into the way people construct their ideologies and theologies lends credence to the kind of crisis counseling that has long been advocated by the evangelical/fundamentalist wing of Christianity. Again, we must remember to evaluate the validity of a concept independently of those who hold it.

THE FRIGHTENING OPPORTUNITY

If praxis proves to be a valid description of how people establish religious convictions, then youth ministers must realize that crisis counseling is crucial for theological formation. The actions taken in resolving life crises must be directed in ways that move young people into commitments to Christ and to theological stances establishing them as Christian believers.

Times of crisis offer youth ministers their best opportunities to help young people become Christians. The danger in this situation is obvious: to mishandle or incorrectly advise a young person in a crisis can establish an anti-Christian ideology that can last a lifetime. But, as in John's case, loving, decisive counsel by a youth worker rooted in Christlike behavior and scriptural truth can turn a young person's life toward the eternal life offered by Jesus Christ.

9 Junior-High Ministry: Too Old Too Soon

Maybe it's their diet. Maybe it's their lifestyle. Whatever the cause, junior-high kids grow larger and enter puberty earlier than their counterparts of previous generations. Junior-high students are growing up faster than ever before. They seem to control their own lives at earlier and earlier ages, to do things that a generation ago were reserved for high-school students.

WHY KIDS ARE GROWING UP TOO FAST

A PERILOUS OMNIPOTENCE

This transformation of junior-high students is the result of many factors, not the least of which is the way their parents live. A significant percentage of early adolescents live in single-parent families, and even those who do grow up in intact families are likely to have both parents employed and therefore out of their homes much of the time. With this diminishing presence of parents in their lives, junior-high students are left with the freedom to do what they want to do, to be pretty much what they choose to be.

This newly found freedom is probably more than most junior-high students can handle, concludes child-development psychologist Erik Erikson.[1] Each stage of the psychosocial development of a youngster, explains Erikson, carries with it certain privileges and responsibilities. He points out that when young people assume privileges and responsibilities that belong to a stage of development that is beyond

119

them, they often become emotionally disturbed and psychologically disoriented. Put simply, junior-high kids often fall apart when they have the freedom to do all the things their parents seem all too willing to allow. Studies show, consequently, that high-school graduates looking back on their junior-high years wish their parents had asked more questions of them and exercised more restraints on their behavior. Such declarations seem strange coming from those who, during junior high, seemed to be constantly trying to get their parents off their backs. But studies indicate that what junior-high students *say* they want is not what they actually desire.

Harvard sociologist David Reisman comforts parents who feel they did an inadequate job parenting their junior-high kids. He argues that social expectations for junior-high students have changed so much that none of us know enough about them to guide our children properly through the precarious, formative early-teenage years.[2] The folkways and mores that guided us older types through the junior-high rites of passage obviously don't apply in today's culture. The world has changed so much in the last quarter century that when our kids accuse us of being out of touch with what's going on in the world, we must humbly confess that they're probably right. Furthermore, most of us don't really want to know what's going on. We want to go on believing that kids are kids and that regardless of what generation they belong to, they're pretty much the same. Yet empirical research on junior-high students reveals that teenagers of this generation aren't like teenagers of previous generations, and that the time-honored directives that guided us through adolescence won't work for them.

THE INFLUENCE OF TELEVISION

Because of diminishing parental guidance, then, junior-high students now get their directives from their peers—and from television. Peer groups exercise great influence on teenagers, but they function primarily as enforcers of values and lifestyles prescribed by the electronic media. Whether we like it or not, television has become a primary socialization agent for teenagers. If junior-high kids deviate from the directives given by what Marshall McLuhan calls the "cool media," their peer groups bring them back into line.

AFFLUENCE

Television and our affluence has combined to give too much too early to too many of our children. This generosity has jaded them. As Muslim pilgrims trek to Mecca, so middle-class kids trek to one of the Disneylands. Presents for Christmas become increasingly exotic, the cost reaching into the hundreds of dollars. A junior-high kid without a ten-speed bike is considered deprived, and the possession of a Walkman is seen as a constitutional right.

The significance of kids experiencing and getting pretty much what their hearts desire can't be underestimated in a consumer-oriented society in which adulthood means being able to buy what we want and go where we please. In this sense, then, junior-high kids reach "adulthood." The only thing that changes with chronological age is that the toys are different.

THE FEAR OF DEATH

Junior-high students are also becoming preoccupied with things we'd rather not have them thinking about—like the fear of death. "Thinking of death," we claim, "is for old people." However, the neo-Freudian scholar Ernest Becker makes it clear in his Pulitzer prize-winning book *Denial of Death* that the awareness of mortality is increasingly breaking into the consciousness of junior-high kids and even younger kids.[3]

According to Becker, life becomes tolerable only because we human beings have developed social mechanisms that blunt the awareness of our own impending deaths. Becker claims that the awareness of our corruptible nature is rushing toward us like a roaring locomotive out of the night, while we lie helplessly bound on its track—a truth most of us find psychologically unbearable. Society usually has been an effective conspirator, hiding this truth from us until in later life our aging flesh forces us to accept our mortality.

Yet during the past few decades, people have become increasingly aware of death and dying. And it's not just old people who think about dying. Junior-high kids who ought to be playing capture the flag and spin the bottle are beginning to think about their own mortality. Becker calls it "a sickness unto death." The awareness of death breaking into the consciousness of junior-high kids may well be the most painful hallmark of our age.

WHAT SHOULD YOUTH WORKERS DO?

While many sociologists and psychologists agree that kids are growing up too fast, a handful of anthropologists contend that kids aren't growing up fast enough. After all, as these anthropologists point out, in most preliterate societies (we don't call them *primitive* anymore), people get married shortly after puberty and take their places in the adult community. In those nontechnological societies where years of formal education aren't required to train a person for his role as family provider or for her role as a wife-mother, kids are married and established as adults by the time they reach what we call the junior-high stage. Furthermore, vocations in preliterate societies are prescribed by tradition that delivers young people from the stress faced by our own young people—who must confront, almost in a kind of existential aloneness, the decisions that determine their destinies.

While the anthropologists educate us with some enlightening cross-cultural perspectives, they offer us little real help. We know that in our society kids would be better off if they didn't become adults until later in life, and that early adulthood can be disastrous. We know that opportunities for kids will be significantly diminished if they marry in their early teens, for such marriages usually end young people's education, and the failure to get an extended education may force them into second-class citizenship.

Even though adulthood shortly following puberty may be functional in preliterate societies, it would be a disaster for the junior-high students in our churches. It's in these straits that youth workers must figure out what to do with kids who must cope with issues that would better be left to a later stage in their lives.

We're finally learning, though with some regret, that all the problems and issues that fit high-school programming a decade ago must now become the subjects for junior-high programs. Dating, sex, personal-identity issues, and the rest have now come to occupy the junior-high consciousness. Perhaps what most concerns us in the evangelical tradition is that decisions relating to personal relationships with Christ occur for the most part in the early teens. Consequently, it may be time for us to recognize that junior-high ministry is most important. By the time most kids reach the senior-high years, many of their behavior patterns may already be set and their decisions about religious matters already made. Waiting to get to kids during their high-school years may be too late.

HELPING KIDS DEAL WITH THEIR FEAR OF DEATH

If Becker is right that teenagers are becoming pre-occupied with thoughts of death—and I think he is—then the days of Bible charades should be over for junior-high fellowship groups. It may be time to figure out how to help teenagers cope with their newest malady—an ominous awareness of their own corruptibility and mortality. It was hard for us to accept the neo-Freudian claim that our erotic nature woke up much earlier in life than we had supposed, but we accepted what we had to accept and made the fact a

123

part of our programming. Now we must grapple with an even more fundamental dimension of neo-Freudian psychology: We must admit that to come of age today brings with it a whisper of death's reality and imminence.

The implications of Becker's thinking are obvious for youth workers—we must begin helping our kids deal with death. It may not be that bizarre at all for your youth group to meet in the parlor of a funeral home as the undertaker explains what he experiences when he confronts the families of those who die. Junior-high kids are morbidly fascinated with the business of burying the dead and particularly interested in what people do and say when a teenager dies. Such discussions will move them to talk about eternal salvation far more than any descriptions of hell or showings of *Thief in the Night*.

Junior-high students try to escape their fear of death by making life frivolous, thereby denying that life is a precious reality that nonetheless moves toward an abyss. No wonder kids goof off with such enthusiasm. Nihilistic existentialism lies dormant in their thought processes; like smooth stones thrown over the surface of a pond, they dance until they run out of momentum and sink into what Kierkegaard called, "a hundred thousand fathoms of nothingness."

They *will* run out of momentum. It may be the result of a classmate committing suicide. It may be the result of seeing a movie like *Platoon*. It may be because of some music they've heard. And when they lose their momentum, they'll be vulnerable to anyone who gives ideological form to their nihilistic state of being.

Youth workers, then, have the task of intercepting these smooth stones before they run out of momentum, so that when they stop, they won't sink into despair. Youth workers must come with the good news—that life does have meaning, that they are significant, and that Jesus has already died to save them from despair. Getting saved makes a lot of sense if Becker is right. Youth workers must simply find ways to get kids saved. The salvation of the gospel is ultimately the only means whereby they can live with triumph in the face of death. Plans for life (vocations), the meaning of love (it isn't just a game), and the authority of Scripture (it holds the story of hope) all become significant in the face of death. In spite of what we'd like to think, junior-high students increasingly live in the face of death. They're older than we thought.

CHANGING THE MEDIUM
OF YOUTH MINISTRY

If it's true that the medium is the message, then youth workers may need to explore new ways to convey the truth to junior-high minds. I'm not convinced that the hour meeting once a week can get them out of their defensive silliness long enough to deal with the sickness of their souls.

How about replacing the weekly Sunday-evening fellow-ship meetings with quarterly or bimonthly junior-high retreats? Getting the kids out of their normative environ-ments and away from the identity symbols that weakly prop up their fragile egos can provide a setting where, in the words of the sociologist Peter Berger, an "alteration of con-sciousness" can occur. On a retreat, removed from the disruptions of TV and the distractions of a typical weekend, junior-high kids can be directed to spiritual things. In *The Social Construction of Reality* authors Peter Berger and Thomas Luckmann help us realize that in such a removed setting, the rest of the world becomes less real, making it more possible for junior-high students to concentrate on things they might otherwise avoid.[4] Such a periodic youth retreat can provide the sociological conditions that Sunday-evening youth fellow-ship meetings seldom approach.

If I had my way, I'd set up a youth retreat for junior-high students at least every other month. I would still have the Sunday-evening meetings for unpackaging the retreat experiences and for revitalizing the emotions and commitments that accompanied those experiences. Getting the money and the time to do what we think is best is not always easy, but we must redefine personal needs and restructure our programming if we're going to relate to a new generation of junior-high kids.

10 Family Ministry:
What Is the Christian Family?

As a presidential candidate, Jimmy Carter announced that if he were elected, he would improve the stability and quality of family life in America. Like most Americans, he saw that something bad was happening to the family, which most of us believe to be the fundamental institution of society. When he became president, Jimmy Carter convened the famous (or, depending on one's political leanings, infamous) White House Conference on Families. This gathering of social scientists, family therapists, and government policy makers was to draw up recommendations for strengthening Americans' commitment to solid marriages and healthy child rearing. Instead of making positive policy suggestions for strengthening American families, the conference became a battleground of conflicting familial ideologies and revealed that the experts had no consensus of values. So diverse were the opinions at the conference, in fact, that the participants couldn't agree even on a definition for *family*.

Those who championed gay rights, for example, contended that two people committed to a homosexual relationship should be defined as a family and should be entitled to raise children. Radical feminists asked that the dyad of mother and child replace the traditional mother-father-child triad. Many argued that those who cohabited outside of marriage should be viewed as being in familial relationships. All in all, the discussions became so confusing that the conference, which originally was to be called the White House Conference on the Family, was renamed the White

House Conference on *Families* (italics mine). This renaming seems to have represented some kind of governmental approval of alternative lifestyles advocated by the liberal/ radical exponents of the New Left and the "secular humanists" so feared by fundamentalists. Indeed, the renaming of the conference made it clear that the definition of *family*, which for so long was tied up with married parents and their children, was actually loose and up for grabs.

THE RESPONSE FROM THE NEW RIGHT

The effects of the White House Conference on Families have been astounding. The alleged experts who participated in the conference established an agenda that prompted a countermove, giving rise to the political New Right. The values expressed at that conference (which in no way reflected Jimmy Carter's personal family values) trumpeted the beginning of war over sexual styles and child-rearing policies of avant-garde social scientists and educators. And the counterattack would make traditional family values the only acceptable values of the land.

While I'm not suggesting that the White House Conference was solely responsible for the pro-family movement or for its expression in the New Right, this conference so elicited the ire of a dormant majority of conservative Christians that they seriously challenged the liberals. Suddenly the Right-to-Life movement seemed omnipresent. The ERA was formidably opposed and unexpectedly defeated. The freedoms of homosexuals were questioned. Sex-education policies of the public school systems came under fire.

In the midst of this reaction to alternative lifestyles, the New Right's leaders raised more questions: Who are these experts who presume to challenge historical values inherent in the Christian family model? What gives these professional social scientists the right to prescribe how children should be raised? Who are they to tell parents they have no right to use corporal punishment on their children or that they must subject their children to sex education prescribed by boards of education? How dare these social-service professionals pressure the government into stripping away parents' rights so that teenage daughters can obtain contraceptives and abortions without parental consent—and at the taxpayer's expense?

The New Right became aware of a group of elite academicians and social workers who had conspired to pilfer more and more of parents' child-rearing prerogatives and deliver those prerogatives into the states' hands. What the conservatives found even worse was that these family experts were secular humanists. The pro-family New Right leaders claimed that these anti-family secularists with their wild ideas about alternative lifestyles had to be stopped or else the traditional family, and the bourgeois democratic society that depended on it, would come to an end.

What the pro-family people especially scorned was the emerging feminist movement. If the movement had not been taken over by its more radical elements, it might have escaped the wrath of such antagonists as Phyllis Schlafly. Most Americans do believe in many of the feminists' demands—equal pay for equal work, for example, and equal employment opportunities for women. The feminists, however, seemed to many to be anti-family. They appeared to put the right of an individual woman's quest for self-realization above any commitment to a marriage or child rearing. It seemed as if the feminists not only justified but lauded those women who walked away from their families to "find themselves." Advocating an ideology that considered heterosexual marriage rape, radical feminists cast a shadow over *all* forms of feminism in the minds of many mainstream Americans.

THE 1980S—A SHIFT IN DOMESTIC BEHAVIOR

In their battles with such ideological foes, the pro-family movement was both a result and a cause of a major shift in domestic behavior in America. During the 1980s, statisticians began noting remarkable reversals in trends that sociologists in the field of family studies had previously thought irreversible. Divorce rates, which had steadily risen since the turn of the century, began leveling off. Studies analyzing the attitudes of collegians toward marriage revealed that they viewed marriage as a positive prospect. Evidences indicated that promiscuous sexual behavior was beginning to abate among middle-class teenagers (due partly to fear of sexually transmitted diseases). Finally, religious ideals for dating and marriage were again gaining legitimacy.

Such reassertions of traditional family values were evident, however, only among America's middle-income families. In the midst of this reaffirmation of bourgeois family values, the American underclass (second- and third-generation welfare people endemically unemployed, unskilled, and usually of socially disinherited minority groups) has departed significantly from traditional, established modes of sexual behavior and family life. By 1990, for instance, more than 90 percent of all births among welfare families in New York City will be out of wedlock.[1] The divorce rate among the poor, which has always been higher per capita than among more affluent social classes, is soaring.

SOCIAL CLASS AND THE HISTORY OF THE TRADITIONAL FAMILY

Which points us to this principle: In any analysis of trends in family behavior, social class plays a highly significant role. What is true within one socioeconomic group may be the opposite of what is true in another. By lumping all social groups together in statistical analyses, researchers can make facts and figures about middle-class behavioral patterns appear worse than they really are. In reality, the traditional, middle-class family and its accompanying sexual values are reviving in America at the very time the underclass is apparently abandoning all semblance of organized family life and sexual responsibility.

I assume that most readers of this book work with young people in the context of middle-class churches and middle-income families. What I have to say, consequently, is relevant primarily to ministry within that particular class.

Just where did the idea of a "traditional" family originate in the first place? Interestingly, the traditional family is not entirely a biblically prescribed notion but a bourgeois invention that manifested itself in the nineteenth century. The good qualities of the traditional family became evident only as a consequence of the changed lifestyles and of the affluence that followed the Industrial Revolution. Historian Phillipe Aries, who best chronicles the development of what we now call the traditional family, brilliantly argues that both the socioeconomic structure of a nonagrarian social system and the intellectual framework of the Enlightenment had to be established before the traditional family, with the lofty functions we assign to it, could be birthed.[2]

The idea that a woman's place is in the home, for example, couldn't exist until the economic system was reconstructed so as to release her from the necessity of working out in the fields alongside the men. In biblical times, it should be noted, women didn't enjoy the luxury of staying home and making the rearing of children their primary occupation. The common women of the ancient world plowed, harvested, gleaned—participating in a host of other economic activities that make contemporary mothers with vocations outside the home seem underemployed by comparison (see Prov. 31). It wasn't until technology spawned the Industrial Revolution and improved productivity that it was possible for women to be free to concentrate on child rearing—news to preachers who claim that women have always made child rearing their full-time occupation. And it was not until later technological innovations—indoor plumbing, for example —refined what the Industrial Revolution began, further improving the quality of domestic life that women could be freed sufficiently to have the time and energy that bourgeois mothering required.

THE FUTILITY OF THE FEMINIST IDEAL

During the last two decades—and especially with the 1963 publication of Betty Friedan's *The Feminine Mystique*—feminists have attacked this privilege of making child rearing a primary vocation, questioning this supposedly traditional role. A growing belief that child rearing kept women from realizing their individuality (a value propagated by the Enlightenment philosophers) caused the new feminists to see homemaking and child rearing as a trap rather than a privilege. Women were made to feel that they could never realize their human potential (another buzz word of the times) unless they found employment in the economic world hitherto reserved for men.

This supposed "escape into the real world" has seldom brought the results women thought it would. To the contrary; most women found they had not so much escaped the drudgery of housewifery as they had entered the dog-eat-dog world of competitive capitalism, complete with labor disputes, office politics, and ulcers. Prejudices against women, furthermore, often prevented their upward mobility into jobs that offered more intellectual challenge, so that a career often meant little more than nodding yes to "Can you type?" More and more women who had forsaken home and family for what they were told was "more fulfilling work" began wondering what they had gotten themselves into. When they reached the age of thirty, many career women began asking themselves if the working world was all they had thought it would be.

Word began to spread that perhaps, just perhaps, they had lost more than they had gained. Even Friedan, that high priestess of feminism for almost a decade, began to have second thoughts about the whole thing. Increasingly, biologi-

132

cal evidence indicated that the hormonal makeup of women motivated them to desire motherhood;[3] and even the famed anthropologist Margaret Meade argued that women were destined by nature to be mothers. Add to this the self-doubts within the feminist movement and the attacks on its ideology from the New Right, and it is no wonder that women began to question the ideology of self-actualization at the expense of family commitments. Although this sounds like a sexist statement, the evidence is clear: Biological factors make mothers the best primary agent of child rearing in early years of development.[4] Young women need to know that many early-childhood specialists believe that it's best for mothers to interrupt their careers during their children's preschool years in order to give them maximum attention.

FINDING A BALANCE

Having played with the extremes in the last couple of decades, our modern cultural milieu is arriving at an almost healthy balance of women's roles. Our society readily acknowledges women's skills and interests that enable them to gain high levels of personal fulfillment through vocational, out-of-home pursuits previously considered men's exclusive turf. At the same time, however, we also readily accept homemaking and child rearing as an exciting and self-fulfilling challenge. Young women in college are more and more willing to admit that their goal in life is to get married and have children. Those who do seek careers outside the home seem increasingly aware that having children means taking time off from their jobs so that they can give full time to raising their children during the preschool years. While more than half the married women with children work outside their homes, an increasing percentage of this group is opting to interrupt their careers until their children reach school age.

We in Christian ministry should applaud this fine balance between career and family. On the one hand, we should encourage young women to use their God-given gifts, heeding the Pauline admonition, "Do not neglect your gift, which was given you" (1 Tim. 4:14a). On the other hand, we must communicate to young women that marriage and children are also excellent options for gaining personal fulfillment and achieving spiritual maturity.

Because America's socioeconomic system has changed so much, men's roles have also been altered. Women's career climbing has established a consciousness of sexual equality among us. Women's demonstrated ability in the marketplace has altered the consciousness of the American people more than anything else. Young men, therefore, must learn to regard women as potential partners, not helpmates. This means clothes washing, food fixing, and sink scrubbing belong as much to husbands as to wives. Child raising, furthermore, is similarly a joint venture. Today's women, highly educated and acculturated into expectations of creative leisure, can't handle confinement that results from trying to raise children without a husband's help. Unless husbands share in the early rearing of their children, young mothers will have little time for the kind of entertainment and cultural enrichment that keeps them emotionally alive and personally happy.

When children go off to school and—as is usually the case—mothers return to their careers, the sharing of domestic responsibilities by parents becomes even more important. Parents need to be available to receive their children home from school and to be involved in their extracurricular activities as well as religious education.

For these relatively new, cooperative roles to have a binding effect on young people, they must be legitimized by religion—and therefore taught within the context of the church. I'm not suggesting that youth leaders look for proof texts that dictate these new cooperative roles for parents, but I'm suggesting that programming for young people include significant time and attention to teaching the biblical basis for the kind of empathetic, mutually supportive marriages described here. I'm aware that young people may not be as interested as we'd like in learning about roles in a Christian marriage, but the absolute necessity for them to gain a proper understanding of such roles is too obvious to be ignored. I'm amazed at how little biblically prescribed role modeling and teaching is carried out by most youth workers. Surely we are called to be more responsible. Youth workers make their finest contribution to the well-being of families when they help young people understand what their religious faith has to say about the playing out of family roles.

THE DANGERS IN FAMILY COUNSELING

Many people suggest that youth workers must do more than teach young people about healthy marriages. Some suggest that youth workers should counsel and educate the entire family. I have some serious doubts about such proposals.

1. Will youth workers who advocate this family approach be in conflict with their senior pastors, who could be threatened by this encroachment into their responsibilities?
2. In their attempt to gain the knowledge necessary for dealing holistically with families, will youth workers be detracted from their specialized training in understanding and dealing with adolescents?
3. Will parents welcome what could easily be understood to be intrusions into their private family lives?
4. Would this whole-family involvement of youth workers erode their ministry as confidants for young people, who might feel that their youth directors are no longer on their side?

Beyond these questions is a more pressing issue: Does *anybody* have enough expertise to help families work out their complicated problems? Sociologists like Peter and Brigitte

Berger and psychotherapists like Christopher Lasch suggest that the credentialed experts in familial studies not only have no cure for family sicknesses but also may be part of the disease. Many prominent writers feel that until somebody can assure us that the self-acclaimed experts know what they're talking about, it may be best to leave family matters in the hands of parents. The individual idiosyncrasies of children are so diverse, these writers suggest, that only their parents—who best know them—can prescribe what is best for them. Furthermore, since what these experts prescribe changes so often and so radically, their prescriptions become exceedingly suspect. It seems strange to me that just at a time when America finally and vigorously questions and challenges so-called family experts, church leaders are proposing that youth workers join the ranks of these experts. Is someone plotting the complete destruction of these harried youth-group leaders?

Perhaps the best way to strengthen American family life is for us to recognize that the reaction to the White House Conference on Families was not simply right-wing political opposition. Perhaps it's time for us to recognize that Americans have the good sense to contend that family life is a private matter and that it's not open to intervention by state or church. We will hear what the experts say, whether they are trained in seminaries or in schools of social work—but in the end we demand to be left alone to raise our children and conduct our family affairs as we wish. We will readily seek out information when we need it, but we'll probably adamantly resist experts—even if they're from the church— who try to sit down in our living rooms and intervene in our private lives. Leaders of the church should always be available to help (although I believe they can help far less than they think they can), but it is not their prerogative to intrude into homes where they are not invited. Church leaders—and especially youth workers—must declare what the Bible prescribes about family life, but they must do so from their traditionally accepted platform. People will come. People will listen. And in the end people will decide how to apply what they've learned. They will accept changes in family models, but those changes must conform to a religiously prescribed ideal. In the end, freedom to work out that ideal is a private affair. In the end, Americans believe not only in separation of church and state but also in separation of church and house.

Youth workers can conduct parenting courses. They can intervene with the law at their side if children are being abused or if spouses are being brutalized. They can be big brothers and big sisters in a single-parent situation. They can counsel. But they had best not presume that they are able or welcome to intervene in the day-by-day affairs of family living.

11 Events:
From the Church Basement to the Arena

The big events are back. Young people are flocking to Jesus festivals, Christian rock concerts, youth congresses, rallies, denominational conventions, and a host of other gatherings. The size of some of these gatherings staggers the imagination: The annual four-day Creation Festival in central Pennsylvania draws more than 40,000, while the Southern Baptists of Missouri packed in over 20,000 for an all-day celebration at a theme park outside of Kansas City.

The phenomenon is evident not only in America but also in England, where 15,000 young people rock and roll to music groups at Greenbelt, a Christian arts festival held in the city of Leeds, and where more than 27,000 get together in the island's northern resort town of Prestatyn for an event called Spring Harvest. Patterned after Spring Harvest, New Zealand's Mainstage draws kids from Down Under. Even in highly secularized Australia and supposedly spiritually dead Europe, massive youth conventions are suddenly in vogue, and Christian rock festivals are often smashing successes.

Youth for Christ is rediscovering the rally. In cities across the country, young people are being drawn to gatherings reminiscent of rallies held in the '40s and '50s. A special genre of youth speakers, now called "great communicators," belt out an old-time religion spiced with Cosby-like humor and a hip vocabulary. After a hiatus of evangelistic methods nurtured by relational theology, Youth for Christ leaders are finding that young people they thought were beyond such appeals are going down the aisles to the strains of "Just As I Am." Even Campus Crusade for Christ has gotten into the big-event act. This organization still makes a one-on-one presentation of the Four Spiritual Laws its mainstay, but it also sponsors youth congresses and conventions.

Mainstream denominations, too, are discovering young people's current fascination with a style of evangelism that seemed all but written off by the late '50s. Conservative Presbyterians, headquartered in Chattanooga, have made a three-day, upper-middle-class gathering called Fun in the Son a major instrument for generating enthusiasm and commitment to the church.

RELIGIOUS WOODSTOCK

It's an oversimplification to define these gatherings as Christian replications of the rock festivals and concerts promoted by the secular community, despite obvious parallels that invite such an easy explanation. Certainly the Jesus festivals (as they have come to be called) look like religious Woodstocks. Creation, Jesus Northwest, Fishnet, and the like are set up, in most instances, outside urban centers—at farms, pastures, and rural parks—and feature religious rock bands on the main stage. Reminiscent of the counter-culture gatherings of the spaced-out, dropped-out generation that replaced the social protesters of the '60s, modern religious attenders camp out, dress in raggedy clothes, and look a whole lot like their predecessors. Religious rock vibrates at every meeting of these festivals, and the crowds scream and gyrate to drums and guitars.

The popularity of the groups that play and sing the new sound of contemporary Christian music has no doubt contributed to the development of many of these festivals. Christian radio stations have elevated groups like Petra and the Imperials to celebrity status. The multi-million-dollar Christian record business has made collectors' items of releases by Amy Grant and Michael W. Smith. Add to this the promotional paraphernalia of T-shirts and buttons and whatnot, and we have on our hands hot rock stars who are often prohibitively expensive to hire. It takes the income from large gatherings to finance their concerts. Whether we're dealing with cause or effect, however, is hard to determine. Did big gatherings become a necessity because of the cost of Christian rock artists, or did Christian rock artists generate the interest for big gatherings?

Before we are tempted to easy comparisons and simplistic parallels, we should note that in some instances these gatherings resemble nineteenth-century camp meetings more than rock festivals. Spring Harvest, the ever-growing English extravaganza, is focused wholly on preaching and teaching and has no special-music groups. Awesome congregational singing rather than soloists lift up hymns to God. Spring Harvest even holds its meetings under a gigantic tent— complete with a sawdust trail.

Obviously, a more sophisticated analysis for these and other big events is needed to explain their sudden popularity.

COLLECTIVE EFFERVESCENCE

Social realists (or social holists, as they are sometimes called in the field of sociology) might be able to lend some interesting insight to the subject of massive meetings. Leaders of this perspective of social reality, from the great modern sociologist Emile Durkheim to the present, have always been convinced that at large gatherings, something happens—something that transcends what the people who make up these events could ever experience as individuals. Durkheim explained that large gatherings of people stimulated to interact in a spirited fashion are capable of producing what he called a "collective effervescence."[1] This collective effervescence, in turn, is likely to compel participants to behave in ways foreign to their individual personalities.

Before we contend that Durkheim and his successors are

describing mere mob psychosis, let me strongly suggest that this phenomenon is much more subtle than we may realize. While social holists don't claim to be mystics, they are nevertheless aware that when individuals interact in some group settings, they collectively manifest traits that transcend the traits inherent in those who make up the group. These collective traits can't be traced to or reduced to the traits of the individuals. Collective traits seem to have a life of their own (Durkheim considered them "things in themselves"), and all the participants integrated with the group are affected by them.

This discovery can be good news to youth workers. According to social holists, certain positive religious traits and beliefs—traits that people greatly need but may be unable to generate on their own—can emerge *sui generis* (of its own kind) in large groups. Faith, for instance, may be hard for some individuals to muster by themselves, but when they are in a group that expresses faith as part of its collective effervescence, they may find themselves full of faith.

Nearly a century ago the American psychologist William James wrote in his classic *Varieties of Religious Experience* that the makeup of some personalities makes them much less capable than others of believing in an invisible God.[2] Faith and other fruits of the Spirit (joy and love come immediately to mind) may be more easily cultivated by collective effervescence than in isolation. In short, a large group can enable certain people to be and do what they might otherwise find impossible. Youth workers who have failed to elicit faith from some teenagers may find that faith comes easily to them at a Billy Graham evangelistic crusade. A bitter young person who experiences neither joy nor love might experience both in the context of a charismatic Jesus festival.

I'm not attempting to reduce the work of the Holy Spirit to a sociological process. I'm only suggesting that the Holy Spirit may be using the collective effervescence of a large gathering of Christians to communicate to particular people.

INFILTRATION FROM THE DARK SIDE

But we can't stop even there. According to biblical admonitions, we should test whether or not the spirit of a group's collective effervescence is of God. The collective consciousness generated at a mass meeting could be diabolical as well as righteous. As a matter of fact, I believe that most theologies of evil have been limited by their proponents' failure to recognize its possibility in these collective terms. Theologians have so concentrated on the individual aspects of demon possession that they often ignore the possibility of evil within the collective effervescence of a group.

History confirms the power of mass meetings to generate an evil and destructive spirit in otherwise benign people. Hitler brilliantly used mass rallies at Nuremberg to foster a demonic mindset in the tens of thousands of people who attended them. Abbie Hoffman claims that Woodstock turned otherwise establishment young people into drug-using, sexually free advocates of a counter-culture. And Jimmy Swaggart has publicly suggested that some rock concerts in the guise of contemporary Christian music are actually instruments of the devil.

Who's to say that Swaggart is wrong? Perhaps the music in a so-called Christian rock concert can elicit a collective *evil* effervescence, even if the performers and the promoters are ignorant of it. Perhaps it's not just a dirty mind that makes some observers of rock concerts sense that the gyrations of the crowd, which are supposed to be a dance unto the Lord, slowly turn into the pulses of sexual intercourse. Why do we agree when a secular philosopher like Allan Bloom (*The Closing of the American Mind*) verifies the evil effervescence of mass musical gatherings, yet call a flamboyant Pentecostal preacher who makes the same claim ridiculously narrow-minded?

Social holists' approach to understanding what goes on in a mass meeting is implied in the work of the nineteenth-century psychologist Carl Jung. That Swiss intellectual giant argued that both good and evil were part of a collective unconscious that all members of a given race possess. What may happen at a mass gathering that's marked by intensive involvement and interaction is this: what's in the unconscious of the participants is drawn out into the open, is made part of the collective consciousness of the group, and is then fed back to the individual participants to be experienced on the conscious level.[3] Spellbinding leaders who play on their groups with words and music, for example, can tap either good or evil archetypes that lie hidden in the subconscious of individuals. Sometimes some of each may be tapped and raised to the surface. At any rate, something spiritually powerful can happen in a massive event.

ON THE BRIGHTER SIDE

It would be misleading not to admit that big events are increasingly popular simply because leaders, sponsors, and promoters know how to make them fun. When thousands of adolescent males and females are brought together, I know (from having observed thousands of them at many of these get-togethers) that they spend a lot of time looking over members of the opposite sex. I don't think that's bad. After all, if we think that it's best for Christian young people to marry other Christian young people, it's no mistake to try to bring them together in religious puberty rituals.

THE PARTY CALLED PASSOVER

Mega-events are commendable for deeper reasons, too. Joyful celebration is a foretaste of God's coming kingdom. That's why the Jews of ancient Israel got together once a year and spent one-tenth of their wealth on a gigantic party called Passover. God's kingdom is better symbolized by a party than by poor people standing in line at a soup kitchen. The God of creation had a Son whom the religious establishment constantly criticized for partying with tax collectors and whores (who may have been more fun to be around than the priests). Joy—and that should certainly include a bit of fun—is something that the Almighty wants for all of us.

When my son Bart was a little guy, I took him to Disneyland. After a wonderfully exhausting day of frontier rides and space rides and jungle rides, I finally broke it to Bart that it was time to leave the Magic Kingdom. "Just one more ride on Space Mountain, Daddy," he begged. When I explained that we were out of time and money, he countered assuredly, "Jesus wants me to have one more ride."

How had he come to this glorious revelation, I asked him.

"Last Sunday when you were preaching," Bart replied, "you said that Jesus feels what we feel. You said that when we cry, he cries. Right?"

I agreed that he had indeed gotten the message right.

"Well," he went on, "doesn't it figure that if he feels what we feel, then when we're laughing and having a good time, he's enjoying himself too?"

I had to agree with the logic of his argument.

"Then," he said triumphantly, "I think Jesus would enjoy me having one more ride on Space Mountain."

Not bad theology. When all is said and done, perhaps the big events happen because kids just enjoy them. And the God who enters into his people vicariously enjoys them, too.

12 Apathy:
A Passionless Generation

Søren Kierkegaard, the Danish theologian/philosopher, once wrote:

> Let others complain that the age is wicked; my complaint is that it is wretched, for it lacks passion. Men's thoughts are thin and flimsy like lace, they are themselves pitiable like the lacemakers. The thoughts of their hearts are too paltry to be sinful. For a worm it might be regarded as a sin to harbor such thought, but not for beings made in the image of God. Their lusts are dull and sluggish, their passions sleepy. They do their duty, these shopkeeping souls, but they clip the coin a trifle . . . they think that even if the Lord keeps ever so careful a set of books, they may still cheat Him a little. Out upon them! This is the reason my soul always turns back to the Old Testament and to Shakespeare. I feel that those who speak there are at least human beings: they hate, they love, they murder their enemies, they curse their descendants throughout all generations, they sin.[1]

Kierkegaard would have been especially hard on the young people of our generation. He wouldn't have dignified their sexual escapades and their drug use by calling them sins. To Kierkegaard, sins were passionate acts of defiance against God. Such intense emotions seem absent in the behavior patterns of contemporary young people. They evidence an apathy in their character and a lack of vitality in their corruption.

Ours is an increasingly passionless generation. Perhaps they have experienced too much too often too young. We have let them encounter reality through the media. We have jaded them with so much artificially generated "excitement" that it has become difficult for them to find anything to be authentically enthusiastic about. Even sex, supposedly one of life's most exotic and thrilling experiences, has been stripped of its mystery in our overly sensate culture.

DISARMED BY PERMISSIVENESS

Herbert Marcuse, the radical sociologist from Frankfort School and mentor to Angela Davis, suggested in his book *One Dimensional Man* that "the establishment" has sculpted an apathetic generation of young people in order to diminish their capacity for political rebellion. Their energies have been dissipated in sexual escapades and their rebellious spirits have been allayed with drugs. Permissiveness in these areas of private deviance, he claimed, has sidetracked them from opposition to the social order.[2]

Social writer Vance Packard lends support to Marcuse's theory. In his book *The Sexual Wilderness,* Packard provides significant evidence that demonstrates an inverse correlation between increases in sexual permissiveness and decreases in activism on college campuses. He claims that as students have been provided with more sexual freedom, they've lost the energy required to protest against the social system.[3]

But Marcuse's explanation is more complex than simply correlating political apathy with sexual permissiveness. He further contended that young people no longer rebel against society because society appears to them as a system fully yielding to their desires. They are given the impression that they can have whatever they want: rebellion against a system that provides whatever they want seems insane. What young people fail to realize, however, is that what they want has been determined for them. They are unaware, according to Marcuse, that they actually have been lulled into a comfortable, sensate, permissive, appetizing form of slavery.[4]

Marcuse pointed out that a society must gratify the

wants of its citizens if it is to keep them pacified. However, if its citizens have wants that the system can't gratify, society will then attempt to make those wants unreal while creating artificial wants to replace them. He contended that our society has been so successful in this plot that people have forgotten what their real wants are.

In such a system, young people are discontented. Yet they don't know *why* they're discontented because they don't know what they really want. They feel no reason to strike out against society or to make demands on society. Since they have everything that they *think* they want, they are unable to focus their discontent on anything specific. Consequently, they turn their discontent on themselves. This inner-directed discontent depletes their psychic energies and renders them apathetic.

Marcuse's theory finds ample support in the advertising techniques of American television. Young people need love, but the media tells them "Canada Dry tastes like love." Young people need to believe in something, but the media preaches that "Buick is something to believe in." Young people need a sense of realness in the midst of an artificial world, but the media assures them that "Coke is the real thing." In case after case, consumer goods—artificially created wants—are offered to the audience as things that can satisfy their real needs. Having these things becomes more important than gratifying the basic emotional needs of humanness. Young people have been deceived into spending their money on "what does not satisfy" (Isa. 55:2).

Still another dimension of Marcuse's explanation of apathy strangely parallels the ethical position of many evangelical Christians. (I say "strangely" because Marcuse was a committed atheist.) He believed that the dynamics of enthusiasm were generated by "dialectical tension." Marcuse believed that vitality, excitement, and creativity are the result of a psychological tension within a person's consciousness. That tension, he believed, results from the inner struggle between the motivations of "the flesh" and motivations of "the spirit." Marcuse, like the apostle Paul in Romans 7, argued that the normative state of a human being is marked by inner struggle.

Marcuse went on to argue that in our modern society this inner tension is being abolished. In our increasingly secularized world, people lack spiritual realities as a part of their consciousness. Marcuse believed that views of human personality provided by philosophical positivism and behavioral psychology have led people to perceive themselves simply as advanced primates lacking anything that could be considered the image of God. One-dimensional people who view themselves only as physical creatures without spiritual dimension lack the tensions that generate the dynamism that destroys apathy.

The parallel found among many evangelical Christians is the same tendency to avoid dialectical tension. Many evangelicals exhaust themselves in a quest to close the theological and ethical circles of their faith, not realizing the dangers inherent in the elimination of what could be authentic spiritual tensions.

THE HOPE IN PHENOMENOLOGY

While Marcuse and company make interesting points, I feel that much has evaded them. As I have looked for other approaches to the issue, I've found some promising insights in a little-noticed school of American social psychology known as *phenomenology*. Phenomenologists blame the apathy of contemporary young people on a culture that they believe has provided inadequate purposes and goals for life.

THE NEED FOR HEROISM AND CHALLENGE

These phenomenologists claim that Western society no longer makes available to young people the kind of heroic roles and vocational challenges that are worthy of their humanity—or to the Christian, worthy of their status as

God's children. They believe that young people have lost their vitality and enthusiasm because there is no longer much about which they can become authentically excited. Few vocations seem to provide young people with a sense of having significantly contributed to the good of humanity and to the destiny of society.

I recently returned from a conference for youth workers in England. In a discussion group I attended, I heard one youth worker after another describe the apathy that exists among the urban poor. "Without jobs," I was told, "young people become dispirited and apathetic." I suggested that cottage industries be started in each church located in these deteriorated and depressed districts. Young people can escape their sense of apathy and psychic emptiness only if they have jobs, and if the existing political-economic structures don't provide those jobs, then the churches should.

Churches could ask entrepreneurs in their congregations to serve as consultants to help young people form small industries that would use church basements as production sites. I urged one Anglican youth leader to get his church to provide the necessary but relatively small amounts of capital funds essential to initiate such small industrial programs.

In this way, young people could be inspired to view themselves as persons who might own and run their own businesses. They would have hope. After all, when people needed medical care, the churches established hospitals. When people needed education, the churches provided schools. When young people needed places for recreation, the churches built gymnasiums. Maybe it's time to realize that if urban young people need jobs, then the churches should help these young people to create them.

BELIEVING IN WHAT WE CAN BECOME

One of the most prominent founders of phenomenological science was the University of Chicago professor George Herbert Mead. In his own day, Mead declared war on the

151

rudimentary forms of behavioral psychology that since his time have come to dominate psychology departments in contemporary academia. Mead's attack was built on his conviction that most psychologists pay too much attention to the role the past plays as they seek to analyze what determines the nature of human personality. He believed that case studies that explain behavior, attitudes, and character strictly as results of past events ignore one of the most important determinants of people—their perception of the future. What people believe they *can become,* according to Mead, is even more important than what they have been.[5] People's hopes and dreams figure more significantly in what they are in the present than behaviorists or neo-Freudians are willing to admit. Those who follow Mead's style of thinking blame the apathy of contemporary young people on a culture that fails to provide goals that challenge them to greatness.

I have found Mead's theories to be applicable in my own experience. Some years ago, I had a student who was the epitome of what is called a "burnout." He was apathetic and disinterested; he took my introductory sociology course and was flunking it solidly. It seemed as if his life was going nowhere. Then, unexpectedly, he turned in an essay that verged on brilliance. I was amazed at his accomplishment and asked him to come to my office for a conference. I told him in very harsh terms that I was angry at him for doing so poorly in my course when he obviously possessed superior talent in social science. I told him that he had the gift for great accomplishments and that he was the kind of student who could earn a doctorate and become a therapist or researcher.

Following that conference, he radically changed. In one semester he went from being on academic probation to being on the dean's list. He went on to graduate school and completed a Ph.D. degree program with honors. The day he defended his doctoral dissertation before his university faculty, he paid me one of the highest honors I've ever received from a former student. He wrapped up his dissertation and mailed it to me with a note: "You earned this more than I did."

What I had done for my student is obvious—I had helped him to believe that he could have a glorious future. I encouraged him to dream about his potential. What he thought he *could become* completely changed his life. His hopes for the future became more important than anything in his past. His dreams and visions gave him a new enthusiasm about life. His apathy was destroyed by a dynamic challenge for his future.

THE CHALLENGE TO GREATNESS

If the phenomenologists are right, then our role as youth workers is clear. We must inspire young people to greatness. By helping young people see themselves as agents of God's revolution, commissioned to a vocation of ultimate importance, we can provide them with a sense of calling that generates unparalleled enthusiasm for life. We can see, for example, the attractiveness and power of the first of the Four Spiritual Laws used by Campus Crusade staff workers: "God loves you and *has a wonderful plan for your life.*" Thousands of collegians have responded to this simple yet compelling declaration that God has unique work for them to do.

We in youth work have mistakenly assumed that the best way to relate to young people is to provide them with various forms of entertainment. For many of us, there is no end to the building of gymnasiums, the sponsoring of hayrides, and the planning of parties. Maybe we should instead invite our young people to accept the challenge to become heroes and change the world.

Fundamentalist churches often serve their young people well by calling them to engage in personal evangelism programs. They lead their young people to believe that by helping people to change into "new creatures in Christ," they will gradually influence the nature of society and change the course of human history. I can remember the zeal that the evangelistic mission generated in my consciousness when I was a teenager. I was convinced that by winning people to Christ, one by one, I was helping to enlist soldiers in a godly army that would soon overwhelm the forces of evil so evident in society. I felt a sense of ultimacy about what I was doing; the purposefulness of my mission left no room for apathy in my life.

Maybe we can't foster social change so simplistically. No doubt we must make structural changes in our institutions or create a new collective consciousness before something of the kingdom of God can be manifested in social history. Even so, it's our responsibility to challenge our young people to become agents for changing the world. By helping them believe that God has called them to participate in the remaking of society, we can inspire them to action and deliver them from the deadness of the spirit we call apathy.

One youth leader I know led her youth-group members into a deep awareness of the sufferings and exploitation of migrant farm workers in their community. These young people invited their state congressman to attend a Sunday-evening youth meeting and explain why he wasn't working to promote legislation that would better protect these migrant workers. When it became evident that he was unwilling to work to improve the lot of the migrant workers, the youth group decided to help his opponent in the next election. The candidate they supported had said that if he were elected, he would introduce legislation to correct many of the evils that caused the migrant workers' suffering and humiliation.

The young people became involved in the ensuing election campaign. They gave out pamphlets, made phone calls, and worked at the polls on election day. They were enthusiastically committed to their task. They bubbled with excitement about the possibilities for victory and greeted with enthusiasm any news of gains made by their candidate.

On election night these young people were at their candidate's headquarters, tabulating results and cheering wildly as victory became evident.

After his election, their candidate remained faithful to his promise. He introduced legislation to correct the injustices inherent in that state's migrant labor system. He actually consulted with the youth group as he drew up the legislation. When hearings on the bill were held, he made members of the youth group part of those hearings. The bill passed and the migrant workers were helped.

What's important here is that these youth-group members had been stirred to vital excitement. Their leader had given them a vision that delivered them from a sense of powerlessness and apathy into a joy and aliveness that is truly spiritual in quality.

ANTIDOTE TO APATHY: SPIRITUAL REGENERATION

While all of these sophisticated explanations of the causes of apathy have some truth to them, I also have my own personal opinion on the subject. Apathy is the natural condition of fallen humanity; it's only on unusual occasions that people are motivated to rise above that entropic state of being. We should be concentrating not so much on the cause of apathy but on what can awaken our young people from their naturally lethargic state to become enthusiastic persons who are intensely concerned about their world, their friends, and God. The apostle Paul considers such aliveness as evidence of the grace of God:

> Because of his great love for us, God, who is rich in mercy, made us alive with Christ even when we were dead in transgressions—it is by grace you have been saved. And God raised us up with Christ and seated us with him in the heavenly realms in Christ Jesus, in order that in the coming ages he might show the incomparable

riches of his grace, expressed in his kindness to us in Christ Jesus (Eph. 2:4–7).

M. Scott Peck, in his book *A Road Less Traveled,* develops much the same theme. Peck, a Harvard psychotherapist, contends that we all are basically lazy and too lethargic to make the life changes that will give us healthy dispositions and personal joy. Peck, like the medievalists, believes that it's only by God's grace that we can have the enthusiasm that dispels apathy.

And what are the sources of enthusiastic activism? We find two primary sources: egotistic self-interest and spiritual regeneration. Our young people need spiritual regeneration, an active work of the Holy Spirit in their lives. The evidence of the Holy Spirit in our age is found not primarily in people who pray in tongues but in people who are wholly surrendered to what God wills to do in their lives. The Spirit gives life! And without the Holy Spirit people are dead—apathetic.

This age, claimed Kierkegaard, can die—not from sin but from lack of passion. I believe that he's right. Passion for life is, ultimately, a gift of God through his Spirit. Let's challenge our young people, and ourselves, to rise from our apathetic morass and claim this most miraculous gift—and with it, God's "wonderful plan" for each of our lives.

PART 3

KEY CONSIDERATIONS FOR EFFECTIVE YOUTH MINISTRY

13 Turnover:
The Revolving-Door Syndrome

Why do many youth workers stay in youth ministry only for a few years? Why do our churches experience a high turnover rate among youth ministers?

We could cite several reasons—conflicts with senior ministers, overly high career expectations, self-image problems, and low pay. But instead of looking at these factors, let's explore four factors I feel are the most significant, yet overlooked, contributors to the turnover rate:

1. Changes in personal theology
2. Personality changes during the maturation process
3. Institutional role conflicts
4. The narcissism of young people

CHANGES IN PERSONAL THEOLOGY

Most youth ministers come out of a fundamentalist ethos. They may ridicule it, condemn it, and negatively critique it, but if they're honest, most will admit they got their start there. This start may have come at a youth rally or a Bible conference. Perhaps it came at a Campus Life or Campus Crusade meeting. It may have come from the personal witness of some zealous Christian friend. Whatever the vehicle, the message probably came in the terms and vocabulary of fundamentalist Christianity.

The intensity generated by the single-mindedness of fundamentalism has its positive side. "Moderate" movements seldom create the kind of enthusiasm evident in movements characterized by absolute beliefs and principles. Eric Hoffer, the longshoreman philosopher, pointed out that extreme beliefs can generate the kind of excitement and fervor that characterizes the "true believer."[1] Hoffer's observation can't be taken as blind support for fundamentalism; my point is that fundamentalism can generate among its adherents a commitment seldom equaled by those with more "moderate" theologies. What fundamentalism can inspire is evidenced in the amazing fact that in 1960, one out of every six American Protestant missionaries was a graduate of Moody Bible Institute.

Youth workers, however, tend to move away from their fundamentalist roots in the course of their ministries. This movement may come as a result of their academic activities. Study may lead them to critique the beliefs and practices that before were left unquestioned. Scholarly analysis of the Bible may lead some youth workers to abandon the doctrine of scriptural inerrancy, exploring the positive dimensions of other forms of religious expression formerly considered "liberal." This type of theological pilgrimage reflects what the German sociologist Max Weber called "an increasing tendency to rationalization."[2]

Weber noticed that as religious movements develop logically consistent theologies and rationally prescribed behavioral expectations, adherents lose the euphoria and excitement that characterized the earliest stages of religious experience. He claimed that religious leaders tend to move away from mystical/miraculous kinds of religion toward ethical/rational kinds of religion. This movement extracts a psychological price. Those who make this transition are doomed to lose their zeal.

I'm not suggesting that ignorance is bliss (although there is some sociological evidence to substantiate this point), nor am I encouraging youth ministers to abandon theological study. I'm only pointing out that as an increasingly rational approach to religious experiences displaces the mystical and miraculous, an emotional deadness inevitably begins, leaving youth ministers with a certain nostalgia for the days when their faith was not so "reasonable." As the rational and analytical youth worker moves away from zeal-creating fundamentalism, something within dies. Burnout can then start.

One of the most significant and honest youth leaders I know told me of an encounter he had with one of his old college buddies, who had recently accepted Christ. Years before, this youth leader had witnessed to his friend and had prayed for his salvation. Yet when he was told that his old friend had come to know the Lord, he felt no emotional response. He feigned excitement and said, "That's really neat." He went on to tell me that as he walked away from that encounter, he almost cried. He wondered what had happened to him. News that years ago would have created hysterical joy now left him cold.

Weber would say he had become too intellectual and analytical about religion. Analysis creates paralysis. If youth ministers are emotionally to survive this disenchantment with fundamentalism, they must discover some new mission that once again can generate enthusiasm and create a sense of urgency. Many Christians have been able to do this, providing us models to imitate. Jim Wallis of the Sojourners fellowship is an example. In his personal journey, he has replaced the concerns of the fundamentalist culture with new concerns that will survive the critiques of more sophisticated and rationalized forms of Christianity. In the place of trying to get people "saved" so that they can go to heaven when they die, Wallis has become committed to preaching a conversion experience that will transform people into agents of social change. His emphasis in no way precludes the promise of heaven for the converted, but it rejects the premise that the primary purpose of conversion is to prepare people for other-worldly blessings. Wallis can still get excited about people getting converted. He can still preach with zeal.

161

He can still vibrate with aliveness, showing no signs of burnout.

Wallis's example doesn't necessarily imply that embracing an ethos that to some may be excessively slanted toward a particular sociopolitical outlook (in his case, "leftist") is the only path available to youth workers who are moving away from a fundamentalist value system. If any lesson can be learned from Wallis, it's that a redefinition of the nature and purposes of conversion can enable youth workers to continue to be committed—radically and enthusiastically— and thus remain spiritually and emotionally alive.

PERSONALITY CHANGES

Many youth workers enter the ministry to satisfy emotional needs that result from immaturity. As they outgrow these immature emotional needs that have been gratified in youth ministry, they find that youth work loses its capacity to excite them.

Some youth workers find youth work a means for gaining adoration from members of the opposite sex. In most circumstances, the youth worker gains high rating as a sex object—and many are excited by that possibility. As I look back on my years in youth work, I recall feeling a certain dizzy exhilaration from having high-school girls "turn on" to me as I exercised what I egotistically considered to be "charismatic leadership." I wasn't particularly good-looking and wouldn't have created any excitement among the adolescent girls in the church had it not been for the aura that surrounds the role of "youth pastor." A decade later the thrill associated with generating erotic reactions from teenagers had dissipated, and one of the emotional payoffs of youth ministry was gone for me forever.

Other youth workers may have a psychological need to exercise authoritarian domination over others. They thrive on having young people depend on them for answers to their everyday problems and questions. They gain delusions of grandeur as they see themselves as the primary shapers of the lives of their youth-group members. As they play out such a role, they receive strokes from adult church members who commend them for taking on such an awesome responsibility as determining the future for the young people of the congregation.

A youth minister I know typifies this syndrome. His youth-fellowship meetings are gatherings in which he dictates the mores and folkways that he believes all Christian young people should adopt. He pontificates on all subjects, from rock music to sexual behavior. He's an excellent communicator and makes his presentations entertaining. In his mind, he knows what's best for the young people of his church, and he feels his kids should gratefully accept what he says. He sometimes allows discussions at his youth meetings, but they are always carefully engineered to come out with conclusions that are in accord with his presuppositions.

This youth minister has a desperate need to play this role, and if he ever outgrows his need to be an authoritarian dominator (which often happens to those who experience growth into Christian maturity) he will find youth work dull and unsatisfying.

This pitfall can be overcome if the youth worker can develop a new basis for ministry. One can gain tremendous gratification in empowering young people to discover their own answers to the problems of life. It's possible for youth ministers to learn to rejoice in watching young people "work out [their own] salvation with fear and trembling" (Phil. 2:12b).

INSTITUTIONAL ROLE CONFLICTS

From a sociological perspective, youth ministers are given the task of socializing young people into the dominant values of the culture. Most church members expect that the church youth group will reinforce the values and role expectations that go with a middle-class American lifestyle.

Church members assume that if youth workers do their jobs, they will turn out "wholesome" teenagers who will go on to the right colleges, take their places in business and the professions, marry the right people, buy lovely suburban homes, and give to the church the kind of loyalty that will make them into good members.

Some youth ministers accept these values and encourage their young people to do the same. In such cases there is a minimum of conflict. What youth ministers are expected to do and what they see themselves as doing are in harmony.

On the other hand, some youth ministers may have other definitions of their roles. They may want to communicate what they see as a radical commitment to Christ and the gospel. They may want to teach the simple lifestyle concept as outlined by writers such as Ron Sider. Others may want to call on young people to give up the affluent middle-class lifestyle prescribed by the media and opt for living sacrificially for the sake of the poor. Some youth ministers may want to encourage their youth fellowship members to critique America from the perspective of biblical justice, with the result that their kids may become critical of the government's policies in Central America or the arms race.

I'm intrigued by how many youth ministers embrace a commitment to radical Christianity while they remain employed within churches that are, by nature, conservative social institutions that legitimate the established social system. In such settings, youth ministers find themselves fighting a constant battle against what they see as "cultural religion." They have a vision of inspiring revolutionaries who will wrestle with the principalities and powers in order to express the kingdom of God. The leaders in their churches, however, are more concerned with how many are attending the Sunday-evening meetings, how well their group compares with other youth groups, and sometimes even how many of the young people become cheerleaders and athletes.

Many times youth ministers must carry out their

struggle alone. They exhaust themselves in trying to communicate a radical biblical faith that is not so much rejected as it is patronized. Often this commitment to what they believe to be authentic Christianity is treated by the senior pastor as a lovely form of idealism that can be tolerated but isn't in touch with the real world. After a while these youth workers may tire and give up.

Far worse is a situation where youth ministers find themselves seduced into being merely recreational directors who entertain the kids with wholesome activities that keep them off the streets and off drugs. These youth workers struggle to hold on to their visions while exhausting themselves in a host of activities that have nothing to do with translating their vision into reality. Such a loss of integrity debilitates these youth workers so completely that they get out of youth work, if for no other reason than to save themselves.

How can youth workers successfully work through their institutional role conflicts? There are no easy answers. However, a vital tool for survival is to develop support groups with other youth ministers who share a similar vision of youth ministry. If such support groups meet often enough and the members provide intense affirmation and encouragement for each other, it's possible to survive the emotional ordeal of being a Christian radical in a conservative institution. Such groups are hard to establish due to schedule and logistical conflicts. However, they are crucial if youth workers are to keep their vision in the midst of role conflict.

NARCISSISM OF YOUNG PEOPLE

Contemporary young people live in a nonagrarian society that doesn't need them. Farmers need children for economic reasons. Children help plow fields, milk cows, harvest crops, and do a hundred other chores. In today's world only 4.5 percent of young people live in agrarian settings, compared with almost 70 percent in 1890.[3]

Contemporary American children have been brought into this world primarily to serve one function: to provide emotional gratification for their parents. Mothers and fathers pour wealth and energy into their children so their children will allow them to share vicariously in their successes and happiness. This puts a tremendous burden on young people. If they fail to be successful and happy, they terribly disappoint their parents. Parents feel like failures if their children don't achieve the cultural standards of success. Today's parents aren't happy unless their children are happy. Perhaps it was easier on young people when all they had to do was to plow fields and to milk cows!

Our child-centered familial system has had other disastrous effects on young people. They expect to be objects of service and sacrifice. They have come to affirm the selfish seeking of personal happiness as their highest obligation. Their culture expects them to be egotistical, and they've met that expectation with enthusiasm. While egocentrism has always been an inclination in human personality, our society has made it a virtue.

It's within the context of this narcissistic culture that youth ministers must do their jobs. What's worse is that they often are expected to cater to this self-centeredness. Too often, parents and church leaders expect youth ministers "to do a lot for the young people." Young people are viewed as objects meriting special attention and as persons the church is obligated to entertain lest the church lose them. Youth ministers are not expected to call young people into a life of sacrifice but rather to help the kids "find themselves" so they can achieve personal happiness. This is hard for thoughtful youth ministers to accept because they know that the call of God is otherwise.

This is not to suggest that followers of Christ will not experience self-actualization and personal fulfillment. Christians *are* personally fulfilled and self-actualized, but these states of psychic well-being are achieved only when they are *not* goals.

I know a young man who quit the football team at his high school because it interfered with an evangelistic outreach program developed by his church. He felt football took up too much time and didn't provide blessings for others. This young man believed that he could find more fulfillment in visiting and serving others in the name of Christ than in playing sports. His parents were shocked and upset, and his friends told him he was crazy. Most disturbing was the fact that his youth leaders condemned his decision. They felt that serving others in the name of Christ was important—but not that important!

In our narcissistic society, young people become self-centered, Christianity becomes a system for achieving self-fulfillment, and many youth leaders become depressed trying to serve the egotistical lifestyle approved for young people in most churches.

Again, we find no easy answers to this dilemma. Youth workers who want to impart the sacrificial ethos of the Christian faith to their young people will need to take a "long-view" approach in their ministry strategy. It will take time to fight upstream against the currents of self-indulgence and to turn the tides of narcissism even a little. Youth workers also will need a support group of like-minded youth ministers to help them work through challenges and difficulties.

The "revolving-door syndrome" in youth work is by no means inevitable. Many youth ministers persevere for decades, and some see real progress in their work. However, if more youth workers are to stay in youth ministry for the long term, the church as a whole needs to take a hard look at the factors that make so many leave youth ministry. After we as a body have a clearer idea of what we are collectively facing, we then need the courage to examine together the role of public ministry, the role of the church in society, alternatives for personal growth, and the true purposes of the Christian pilgrimage. If we commit ourselves to this agenda, in concert with supportive peers and sympathetic leaders, we *can* begin to put a wedge in the revolving door.

14 Staff Relationships: The Will to Power

Friedrich Nietzsche, one of the founders of atheistic existentialism, contended that a basic drive governing human behavior is "the will to power." People in youth ministry must, on careful reflection, admit that Nietzsche was right. We know that the will to power expresses itself in a variety of ways in the ongoing affairs of church life.

Youth ministers must face their own tendencies—and the tendencies of their coworkers—to play power games as they try to be "successful" in their vocational calling. Youth ministers sense a need to exercise power as they implement program designs, serve others, and define their identities. And when they do, they enter into conflict with their coworkers.

CAUGHT IN THE MIDDLE

The struggle to cope with church politics is aggravated by the fact the role of "youth minister" is, at best, an ambiguous role. The attempts to professionalize youth-ministry roles have never really worked. Even though youth ministers have tried to define their roles as equal partners with senior ministers, they're still considered "junior ministers" who will one day grow into "real" ministers with "real" congregations. It makes no difference what's written on the organizational charts; the way a congregation sees youth ministers defines their status and identity, often in ways very different from what they deserve. Senior ministers with whom they serve may attempt to define them as copastors, but in functional reality these efforts fail. Congregations almost always will define one member of any given church staff as the "senior" minister, and concomitantly, all other staff members as subservients.

Congregations, despite assurances to the contrary, hold their senior ministers responsible for what happens with the youth groups of their churches. This means that part of the success sought by the senior minister is tied up in how well the youth programs are going. Senior pastors may glibly say at staff meetings that "numbers are not important," but that doesn't alter the fact that large and hyperactive youth groups are prerequisites to their own images as successes. All the talk about the *quality* of relationships with the young people being more important than the *quantity* attending meetings is likely to be greeted with the words, "Yes, but . . . " In their will to power, many senior ministers may unnecessarily pressure youth ministers to get more young people to attend youth meetings.

THE POWER GAMES YOUTH MINISTERS PLAY

Youth ministers are not without guile. They want power, too. And in their will to power, they often play games designed to undercut senior ministers. These games are varied and ingenious.

INTELLECTUAL SUPERIORITY

The first game tries to upstage the senior ministers by demonstrating intellectual superiority. Usually, youth ministers have graduated more recently from divinity schools and Bible colleges, allowing them to appear more up-to-date in their theological perspectives, particularly their ideas about the mission of the church. Youth ministers often play the "Have-you-read-such-and-such?" game in which they cite the latest works of Moltmann (if they're liberals) or J.I. Packer (if they're conservatives). In most cases, their senior pastors have been so tied up with the bureaucratic adminis-tration of their churches that they haven't had the time to read the latest books. Youth ministers easily intimidate the senior pastors with what they know. Knowledge enhances the status of its possessors, and we all know it. Therefore, in their will to power, youth ministers find it hard to resist the temptation to show off their theological prowess.

This power game is played in another arena as well. Sometimes youth ministers conduct Bible studies and train-ing sessions in a way that contrasts their own sophisticated knowledge with the "loving but simple-minded teachings" of their bosses. They threaten the power positions of their senior pastors by getting their congregations to realize that they know more than the senior pastor knows.

THE "PROPHET VS. PRIEST" GAME

Another power game youth ministers play might be labeled the "prophet vs. priest" game. In this game youth ministers cast the senior pastors as people who are more interested in perpetuating the *status quo* than in being "relevant" to the needs of society. This ploy is bound to be effective because the longer pastors serve congregations, the less inclined they are to address controversial issues. Sermon references to such subjects as the arms race, the U.S. involvement in Nicaragua, feminist concerns, and the call to radical discipleship—particularly from a "liberal" perspec-tive—become rarer as the years of the pastorate grind by. In contrast to this, youth ministers cast themselves as daring prophets who are willing to risk all in faithfulness to God.

Youth ministers in fundamentalist churches play this same game with a special evangelical twist. They present themselves as "on-fire soul winners" with a real zeal for the lost, in contrast to the "old guys" who seem, in the words of Max Weber, "to have had their charisma routinized by the demands for rational organization typical of religious institu-tionalization."[1] In this version of the game, senior pastors are cast as people who have lost that "something special" that the young whippersnappers still have. Youth ministers sometimes cast the senior pastors as gutless leaders who don't want to risk offending some of the important church people, while they present themselves as fearless, unintimidated declarers of God's Word.

DENOMINATIONAL BIG SHOTS

Denominational activities provide still another arena in which youth ministers sometimes try to outdo their senior pastors. The youth ministers, for instance, volunteer to serve on one of the committees of their local synods or presbyteries, where they gain a reputation that their senior pastors find very threatening. By becoming "big shots" in their denominations, youth ministers can create the impression that they have fantastic leadership ability readily recognized by those outside the local church, but not by their senior pastors. Furthermore, they may imply that they would be able to do great things in their local churches if only the old guys wouldn't keep them down. This enhancement of their status tempts youth ministers to assume power over their senior ministers.

WHY SENIOR PASTORS ARE ANXIOUS

Senior pastors are not oblivious to these power plays. Their survival as leaders of complicated bureaucracies has depended on their finely honed ability to ferret out and neutralize threats to their power positions. They know they are held accountable for everything that goes on in their churches, regardless of what the deacons and elders say. They know that the simple misfunctioning of some trivial aspect of their church program can ruffle members and cause losses in membership. They *expect* to spend countless hours "putting out the fires" that are set by unsuspecting church workers and members of their staff. Furthermore, they know

172

that the best thing they can do is to so control church life that most fires never start in the first place.

Youth ministers who are innovative and who exercise charismatic leadership can make these senior pastors very nervous. The senior pastors realize that new programs and charismatic leadership often stir up reactions (start "fires"), and senior pastors are aware that such reactions can be troublesome for their preciously guarded ecclesiastical organizations.

Once again Max Weber—the sociologist who above all others made the study of church leadership into a science—provides some basic insights into these institutional conflicts. In his classic book *The Theory of Social and Economic Organization,* Weber makes it clear that charisma is always a threat to those who are trying to maintain "rational" organizational structures. Rational structures demand predictability and control, while charismatic leadership creates unpredictable elements in the system and threatens the possibilities for control.[2]

But we fail to understand the anxiety of many senior pastors if we limit our investigation of church power struggles to sociological factors alone. Psychological factors influencing their will to power often loom even larger in these power games. Ernest Becker, in his neo-Freudian analysis of human personality set forth in his book *Denial of Death,* points out that all of us seek immortality by replicating ourselves in those who come after us.[3] Fathers and mothers strenuously commit themselves to making sure that their children are just like them. Teachers thrive on the hope that their students will become their successors and will carry on to the next generation their thoughts and visions. And it's not surprising to discover that senior pastors hope to see their visions of the church and their theological perspectives replicated in their youth ministers, whom they often treat as protégés. Perhaps more than any of them are willing to recognize, senior pastors may view their youth ministers as instruments to

173

carry out their dreams and hopes after they themselves have left the scene. Becker points out that the subconscious urge of leaders to achieve immortality by being replicated in their protégés was illustrated in the interactions of Sigmund Freud and his prime student, Carl Jung. When Jung began to show signs of establishing an intellectual tradition different from that of his mentor, Freud became so distressed that he fainted. The thought of losing Jung as an instrument to carry on his life's work was intolerable.

Even as Freud couldn't tolerate Jung's deviance from his vision, so senior ministers may not be able to tolerate youth ministers' deviance from their visions and hopes for ministry. Senior ministers sometimes unconsciously crush their youth ministers' ideas and innovations while imposing their own beliefs and hopes instead. The desire to impose their wills on those who work with them increases dramatically if the senior minister senses the nearness of his or her own death. In short, the struggle to dominate their youth ministers and to make them into replications of themselves may be the result of the senior minister's latent longing for immortality.

THE BALANCE OF POWER ON A THREE-MEMBER STAFF

When the professional leadership staff of a church numbers more than two persons, the matrix of relational problems increases geometrically. George Simmel, the founder of the school of thought called "form sociology," clarified how quantitative changes in the leadership elites of churches inevitably lead to qualitative changes in the nature of interactions within the ruling elites.[4] Simmel was particularly interested in what happens when the group increases in size from two to three members. He pointed out that the third member of a church staff can function in a variety of ways.

First, *a third party can play the other two parties against each other and in the process gain power for himself or herself.* For example: The pastor and the associate pastor of First Presbyterian Church are not getting along. Each has enlisted a base of support among church members, but neither has sufficient strength to force the resignation of the other. Then there's Mike, the new youth minister. In a seemingly noble manner, he has refused to take sides in the conflict. In reality, Mike has developed a support base among the church members; both the pastor and his associate realize that Mike holds the balance of power in the church. Consequently, Mike is in a position to get anything he wants and do anything he wants for his youth ministry. Both the pastor and his associate are reluctant to challenge Mike because each fears that Mike might side with the other person. Mike grasps this situation and exploits it for his own gain.

Second, *a third party can take sides in a conflict between the other two parties and thus bring about the defeat of the isolated party.* Rich is minister of music at Glory Christian Church. He's a remarkable person with unusual talents. Scores of young people have come to the church to sing in his youth choir. Rich does an outstanding job with contemporary Christian music, and the youth choir is in great demand. On most Sunday evenings the choir sings in other churches. This means that many young people and their parents miss the evening services at Glory Christian Church. This greatly angers the pastor, who feels that Rich is upstaging him. Furthermore, the pastor doesn't like contemporary Christian music and wishes that Rich would use more traditional music for worship services. But Rich is stubborn and somewhat egotistical. He persists in selecting the kind of music he wants, knowing that the congregation is, for the most part, supportive of him.

Into this conflict steps Joan, the new youth pastor. She discovers that the music program also interferes with her youth program. Young people are singing with the youth choir in other churches on Sunday evenings, which hurts attendance at her youth-fellowship meetings. Furthermore, she recognizes that the young people are more impressed with Rich than they are with her. Joan sides with the pastor against Rich, and eventually Rich is forced to resign. Both the pastor and Joan are delivered from the specter of an overly important minister of music, but the church has lost a crucial part of its ministry.

Third, *a third party can be a reconciling agent who facilitates peace and smooth interaction between the other two parties.* The pastor and the minister of visitation at the Asbury United Methodist Church are constantly struggling over their respective spheres of influence. They are particularly at odds over who is responsible for hospital visitation. Each wants to be "in charge." When Mary becomes the youth minister, she recognizes that in spite of their differences, each of these men views the other with respect and appreciates the other's gifts and dedication. Mary begins to tell each of them good things the other has said about him. She helps each of them to realize that his colleague does view him positively. Consequently, these two men begin to experience attitude changes. They never do settle the question of who is "in charge" of hospital visitation, because they come to like each other so much that they are able to carry out this task together.

There's no doubt that as Christians, we'll want to opt for this third alternative proposed by Simmel. Although we may be tempted to choose one of Simmel's first two options, we know that if we act that way, we sin.

THE ALTERNATIVE TO POWER

Sociologists have long recognized a significant alternative to power. That alternative is *authority*. By power, sociologists mean the ability to coerce (to get others to do our will, even if it's in conflict with their own wills). By authority, they mean the ability to elicit positive voluntary support for our will from people who sincerely believe that we have the legitimate right to ask for their support. Youth ministers, then, have an alternative to power: growing in authority and turning from the temptation to gain power through manipulative games. Choosing to grow in authority rather than to exercise power is not always an attractive option for youth ministers because they know that gaining authority requires sacrificial service and self-giving.

The Bible provides an interesting case study in the way God calls us to abandon power games and become servant leaders with authority. In the first-century Philippian church, power struggles arose between its leaders, Euodia and Syntyche. The apostle Paul, trying to bring peace to that troubled congregation, advised these leaders to follow the model of Christ in their relationships with each other and to give up the will to power. He admonished them to take on "the mind of Christ." In Philippians 2, Paul pointed out that as church leaders these two women should, like Christ, be willing to empty themselves of power and glory, become humble servants, and abandon efforts to make reputations for themselves. Paul went on to point out that it was through assuming the role of sacrificial servanthood that Christ earned for himself the authority he now has with us. Paul urged all church leaders to do the same.

In this chapter I've exposed some of the power games and manipulative techniques we use in our interactions with peers, senior pastors, and lay members of our churches. And we have heard the biblical call to abandon manipulative techniques and to become servant leaders, regardless of how "impractical" this may be. We are to give up the will to power and become ministers who, like Christ, possess authority established through sacrificial service. Each of us must commit to helping others fulfill their high callings in Christ Jesus. Each of us must seek to enable the members of our churches to realize their own potential for living out the dreams and hopes that God has given them. Only if we are willing to lose ourselves in service for Christ and for others will we ever find ourselves and realize all that God means for us to be.

Is what I am suggesting impractical? Perhaps. Politically naïve? Without a doubt. Potentially suicidal to our hopes of ecclesiastical "success"? Possibly. Yet is it not also the very path Jesus himself took to the cross? Yes—and that, ultimately, is the point that matters.

15 Money:
The Seductive Mistress

Following a lecture at which a leading advocate of the radical, simple Christian lifestyle presented his ideas, a heated argument broke out. The speaker was challenged by a listener who contended that prosperity and wealth were rewards that God gives to those who live according to his will. The speaker, on the other hand, argued that the essence of being Christian was becoming radically committed to Jesus' words in the Sermon on the Mount. Such commitment, contended the speaker, required that followers of Jesus live simply and use all surplus wealth to feed the poor and to minister to the oppressed.

After the argument had gone on for almost an hour, the critic said to the speaker, "I realize that we're not going to settle this question today, but it's good to know that in spite of our differences we both worship the same God."

The speaker thought for a moment, then answered, "I don't think so."

"THE GOD OF THE POOR" IS NOT "THE GOD OF THE RICH"

The way in which we understand God is highly influenced by our economic status. The possession of (or lack of) money highly influences what we believe about the nature of God. The lecturer was poor and had one concept of God. His critic, who was rich, had a very different concept of God.

The poor see God as one whom they can call on to provide help against the outrageous fortunes of existence. He provides miracles when people are sick or need economic assistance. He helps them find things that are lost, helps them get jobs when they are unemployed, and provides guardian angels to watch over their children. "The God of the poor" is a champion who sides with them in their struggles against those who dominate their lives.

Ron Sider, in his now-famous book *Rich Christians in an Age of Hunger,* argues that God identifies with the poor in their struggles for economic justice and political liberation. Sider claims that wherever oppressed people crave dignity, hope, and deliverance from grinding poverty, God is present there too. God identifies with the downtrodden and fights for them against the enslaving effects of living in a societal system constructed to serve the interests of the rich.[1]

James Cone, one of America's foremost proponents of black theology, makes this startling statement: "Jesus is a nigger, and anybody who wants to be a Christian must be willing to become a nigger with him." Cone doesn't mean that Jesus was a black man. Being a "nigger" is not simply a matter of skin color. A nigger is a person who is despised and rejected by the world.

Cone may be right. A careful reading of Isaiah 53 and an examination of Christ on the cross provide ample support for his contention. If Cone is correct, to be Christian is to identify with the despised and rejected of the world and to view reality from their perspective.

The middle and upper classes, on the other hand, see God much differently. These people tend to believe that their economic good fortune is the result of their hard work and entrepreneurial skills, and they see God as one who keeps records of the achievements of his people and rewards them according to their labors. The middle and upper classes are convinced that heaven is stratified. Those who did the most for God during their sojourn on earth will be at the top of

that system, while others who were not diligent in service for
the Lord will barely make it through the pearly gates.

The middle and upper classes claim that salvation is by
grace, but they are also convinced that status in heaven can
be improved by good works. These people love the parable of
the talents because in it the hard-working servants who
invest their resources and produce a 100 percent profit are
blessed, while those who produced nothing are cast into the
"darkness, where there will be weeping and gnashing of
teeth" (Matt. 25:14–30).

The affluent members of our society seldom discuss that
other parable in which the owner of a vineyard hires several
people at different times during the day, but at the end of the
day pays each of them the same wages (Matt. 20:1–16). That
parable reeks of the Marxist idea that calls for a proletarian
economic system in which "each will be required to work
according to his need." To the middle and upper classes,
God often functions much like a cosmic business executive
who rewards people according to what they have earned.

Above all else, the affluent see God as rational. He
maintains an orderly system. He is a God of law and order,
and his people can learn rules that will guarantee them
wealth and success. Their theologies are systematic outlines
of how God's system works—and how they can "work the
system."

For the affluent, God legitimates the political-economic
order in which they have so happily established themselves.
Whereas the poor identify with God's intolerance of unjust
social systems and his call to struggle against the principalities and powers (Eph. 6:12), the middle and upper classes
identify with God's warning that those who challenge the
political-economic leaders of the system are opposing God
(Rom. 13:1–5). The affluent see a God who supports the
ruling establishment and condemns opposition to the societal
system as a sacrilegious act.

I was recently the commencement speaker for an upper-middle-class Christian college that prided itself on its evangelical tradition. The president of the school remarked that the graduates of this school were desirable members of society. He pointed out that businesses preferred his school's graduates. He was confident that these graduates would successfully fill a host of important and prestigious positions within society.

I resisted the temptation to start off my speech by saying that if this college was really Christian, the president's remarks would not be true. None of the established social institutions would want graduates from this school if they were Christlike persons. Businesses would be threatened by graduates who challenged their unethical practices. The medical profession would not welcome graduates who criticized the exorbitant fees that make medical care inaccessible to many people. Many law firms would not be attracted to graduates who were interested only in delivering justice. In short, institutions and their leaders would not be favorably disposed to a host of young Christians who, like their predecessors in the early church, had earned the reputation of being people who "turned the world upside down" (Acts 17:6 LB).

Both "the God of the poor" and "the God of the affluent" can be found in the Bible. The cause for these divergent explanations of how the Bible describes God doesn't lie in contradictions inherent in the Scriptures: rather, it lies in the opposing world views of these two different social classes.

We are all aware of the fact that different cultures influence people to interpret the Scriptures differently. How tenth-century monks interpreted a Bible passage was far different from how twentieth-century American theologians interpret the same book. It comes as no surprise to learn that people in the first century read into the Book of Revelation meanings that were far different from those held by people raised in the 1950s and '60s.

What is not always recognized is that rich people often interpret the Scriptures differently from poor people. We readily recognize that biblical understanding is highly influenced by the reader's cultural background, but we ignore the influence of the reader's economic status on how he or she reads the Word.

MONEY AND THE YOUTH WORKER

How then does money influence the mindset of the youth worker? From what already has been stated, it ought to be clear that money influences a person's theology. Furthermore, the youth worker's perception of God will change as his or her economic status changes.

It's interesting to chart what happens to ministers who climb the ladder of ecclesiastical success and experience significant improvements in their financial condition. Usually the improvements in financial status occur gradually so that the "alterations of personality" (as Peter Berger would call them) are hardly perceptible. Adaptations to a different lifestyle occur so slowly that changes in cultural orientation, taste, perspectives on life, and theology are rarely noticed.

During the economic transitions experienced by most youth workers, the prophetic dimensions of their messages, which marked those stages of ministry in which they were poor, are gradually shed. In place of a prophetic message, they develop a religion that emphasizes social adjustment. Whereas these youth leaders once hoped that the members of their youth groups would become nonconformists who would change the world, these increasingly affluent youth leaders begin to promote a religion that supports the established social order. In place of a message that calls for the transformation, if not the rejection, of society and that calls Christians to challenge the evils inherent in the societal system, the increasingly affluent middle-class youth leader encourages young church members to take the steps to become successful members of society.

183

These changes in philosophy and practice merge comfortably with the expectations of many churches, where youth leaders are expected to socialize young people into the dominant values of the culture. Such a mentality is far removed, however, from the revolutionary disposition that often characterized those early Christians whose world view and lifestyle were not characterized by wealth and prestige.

The most difficult position for a youth minister is to be economically disadvantaged while serving in a relatively affluent church. The youth minister, unencumbered by wealth, is likely to have visions associated with radical discipleship patterned after the teachings of Dietrich Bonhoeffer. He or she is likely to have dreams of a church committed to social justice. Continuing to live at a low economic level also means that this youth worker's outlook is less likely to change over time. On the other hand, the church, composed of relatively affluent people, may be socially conservative with a view of discipleship that approximates middle-class respectability. The church members may tolerate the radical youth minister and even think of his or her views as "cute" (albeit immature). However, such attitudes can leave the youth leader feeling that he or she is not being taken seriously. In some cases, particularly where the youth minister has been effective and has inspired the young people of his or her church to radical Christian living, there may be belligerent opposition to the youth minister and even demands for his or her resignation.

BEATING THE MONEY TRAP

To quote the late Dr. Francis Schaeffer: "In the face of these things, how shall we then live?"

While I believe that social and economic factors *influence* a person's understanding of God and the Scriptures, they do not *determine* that understanding. I believe that the Holy Spirit can break into any culturally or economically conditioned mindset with revelation from the heavenly Father. As

God breaks through to each of us with his will for our economic life and practice, we must pledge *now,* before our circumstances change and begin to cloud our judgment, to live by the socioeconomic model revealed to us through Scripture and the Holy Spirit.

Certainly we should resist having our theology and orientation toward ministry determined by monetary factors. That is easier said than done, however. The challenge is to maintain what we believe to be true as our socioeconomic situation changes (usually upward) and its influences on us increase. Let me share three examples of how this kind of maintenance is being accomplished:

●Four youth ministers who serve in the same county in a Midwestern state have pledged themselves to a simple lifestyle and to a radical stance for social justice. They meet once a week for breakfast so that they can affirm their commitment and provide for each other what sociologists call a "plausibility structure" or primary group (see chapter 3). Without the discussions, prayer, and Bible study they have together, their commitments would weaken and their beliefs would become unreal. This support group proves to be a countervailing influence that helps them resist the seduction of their churches and the effects of their own improving money-making situations.

●A youth minister in Florida spends half of her annual vacation serving at a mission station located in Haiti. The shock, upset, and consciousness raising that accompanies these periodic trips to that community of oppressed people helps her cope with the mindset that accompanies her own rise in income.

●John Wesley, the founder of Methodism, recognized the ways in which growing wealth alters religious convictions and had this bit of advice: "Religion must necessarily produce both industry and frugality, and these cannot but produce riches. . . . We ought not to prevent people from being diligent and frugal: we *must* exhort all Christians to gain all they can, and to save all they can . . . in order to give all they can."[2]

However we do it, it must be done. If support groups, trips to third-world countries, and giving away wealth to the poor do not prove to be viable options, then we must find some other way to counteract the seduction of wealth in our consciousness. We must struggle to keep from conforming to the pattern of this world (Rom. 12:1–2). Our views of God and our ministry should be governed by the reading of Scripture under the guidance of the Holy Spirit. Our views should not be determined by money. Overcoming the effects of our improving financial status is essential if we are to be faithful servants of God.

16 Spirituality:
The Price of Pragmatism

It should come as no surprise that Christian youth ministry and spirituality can seem to be mutually exclusive terms. The American religious mind on the whole is biased against spirituality. Americans aren't impressed with spiritual disciplines. We have nothing against them; it's just that we have more practical things to do.

If we value spirituality, we value it for its utilitarian effectiveness. We recognize that prayer changes things, but we seldom view prayer as an end in itself. Prayer is promoted as an essential ingredient for the success of any religious program or project, but it is rarely appreciated as an exercise in holiness.

Similarly, fasting has become foreign to the lives of most American church leaders—including youth workers. When asked about fasting, most of us might respond, "What good will it do?" We might see fasting as valuable when used as a form of protest. We sympathize with political prisoners who starve themselves in their prison cells; we applaud in our movie theaters when Ghandi fasts until his followers abandon violence as an instrument of revolution. But fasting to express the triumph of the Spirit over the desires of the flesh or to enhance spirituality seems a bit weird.

THE ROOTS OF PRAGMATISM

How, we may ask, have Americans become such spiritual pragmatists? Two distinct movements have had a

187

key impact on the direction of our collective spiritual development.

HISTORY
Protestantism is rooted in the German academic community. This fact is important when we consider why devotional meditation and spiritual disciplines seem secondary in our tradition. *Geist,* the German word for *spirit,* is also the German word for *intellect.* Consequently, the enhancing of spirituality within Germanic religious orientations has generally been associated with intellectual processes. When those of us imbued with this Protestant mindset (and America is the center of Protestant Christendom) try to develop "depth" to our religiosity, we usually read books or attend conferences. We readily testify how these books and speakers influence our beliefs and lifestyles, but few of us testify to having been transformed by prayer, meditation, and devotional time.

PSYCHOLOGY
Ever since William James published his classic work *The Varieties of Religious Experience,* the academic world has tended to label those who crave spirituality as "sick-minded." William James's phenomenological approach led him to categorize as abnormal those who become aware of their corrupted and sinful condition and who long to be delivered into a state of holiness.

James's perspective has permeated our culture. We typically assume that "healthy-minded" people are busy activists who seldom experience either the agonies or the ecstasies associated with spirituality. Our preference for "well-balanced" personality types in the religious community is firmly rooted. Most churches are not likely to hire youth workers who claim to have personal discussions with God, see visions, or receive revelations. Most theological seminaries use personality tests such as the Minnesota

Multiphasic Personality Test to ferret out students who hear voices or see apparitions.

It's interesting to note that the apostle Paul would probably flunk the psychological entrance examination given at Fuller Seminary or at Eastern Baptist Theological Seminary. Paul claimed private revelations (Acts 9:3–9; Gal. 1:12), gave evidence of multiple personality syndrome (1 Cor. 9:19–23), and demonstrated symptoms of messianic complex (Phil. 1:21–30). How could he be admitted to our ministerial training programs?

While we must prevent psychotics from assuming leadership positions in our churches, we must also be aware that in our vigilance, we may be excluding those who really *do* talk to God and bathe in the ecstasy of his presence. In our sophisticated caution, we may be shutting out those people who are the spiritual among us.

THE PRICE OF PRAGMATISM

Our cultural emphasis on pragmatic activism and rationalistic psychology has had dire effects on Christian leaders. The first and most important negative result of lack of spirituality is the phenomenon called "burnout." We repeatedly hear of people who drop out of youth ministry because, according to the reports, they exhausted themselves by working too hard. I find these reports difficult to accept. I don't doubt that those who drop out are emotionally drained; but in most cases, the malady can be traced to spiritual causes rather than physical exhaustion. It sounds nobler to say that a given youth worker collapsed because he or she was too self-giving in Christian service than to say the person's emotional dissipation was due to failure to spend time in developing spiritual character.

In fact, a look at some of the hardest-working, most self-sacrificing saints of the church reveals that their attention to the inner as well as the outer religious life gave their lives a zest and sparkle unaffected by their workloads. John Wesley

189

and a few of his friends at Oxford University formed what they called "The Holy Club." This small group met each morning at five for prayer and devotional meditation. They carried on this practice so methodically that they were labeled, in derision, the Methodists. John Wesley was renowned for his staggering workload; yet those who knew him were amazed by his vigor. Mother Teresa spends several hours each day growing in the Spirit. She claims that the Spirit gives her life and vitality. Those who know Mother Teresa say that her zest for life is testimony to the fact that the energy she expends in the spiritual disciplines provides ample protection against burnout.

The second negative result of our neglect of spirituality has been the loss of our ability to impact our culture effectively. We have overlooked the fact that what we *are* as Christians has as much, if not more, influence than what we *do* in establishing the spiritual tone within our nation. Henry Steele Commager, a renowned American cultural historian, comments in his book *The American Mind* that our nation has seldom been *less* influenced by its churches, despite the fact that today a greater proportion of our population belongs to churches than ever before in our history.[1] Jesus told us that we are to be the salt of the earth; but he went on to remind us that if salt loses its taste, it's worth nothing (Matt. 5:13). Jesus is telling us that the quality of our being—which is determined by the quality of our spirituality—impacts our society.

If one of our primary responsibilities as youth workers is to challenge the young people in our groups to influence their world, perhaps it's time for us to review our strategies. Maybe what the typical high school needs is not more rah-rah evangelistic programs but the mere presence of leaders who possess a mystical character because of their immersion in the Holy Spirit through prayer and devotional meditation. Perhaps kids who think the thoughts of Christ, whose very presence radiates goodness, can make a greater difference in the youth subculture than the sum total of all the programs we can glean from youth program books.

I remember a boy who lived in our neighborhood after having spent his earlier years in a convent in Mexico. I sensed something different about this boy—something that went far beyond his Hispanic identity. He had an unexplainable serenity about him. When he walked with us to school, something unusual happened to us. We were a bit subdued and even felt uncomfortable. We told no dirty jokes and used no vulgar words when he was with us. At the time, I was already a converted, evangelical Christian, and I had often told my friends I was offended by their off-color stories and obscene words. They never changed because of what I said or did, but this strange Mexican boy was able to influence them for good in a way that none of us could understand. What he *was* had far more impact than what I said or did. The nuns at his Mexican convent had taught him to be spiritual.

As I remember that Hispanic boy, I've often wondered if most of us would want him in our groups. We want our young people to be moral, to respect their parents, to avoid sexual compromises, to be active in evangelistic concerns, and to be committed to social justice, but do we really want them to be spiritual? Do we want them to become persons who delight in solitude and extended prayer? Do we want them to possess a grace and peace that would detach them somewhat from the superficial attitudes so typical of the high-school subculture?

WHAT ABOUT US?

Perhaps because we are fearful of spirituality, we know we can't program the Spirit, and we're threatened by what we can't control. The work of God in our kids' lives, and in our lives, may very well pull us out of the cultural mainstream. It may require a radical restructuring of our life priorities. Are we willing to get on our knees and fall in love with God? Are we ready to lie prostrate at the altar for hours, waiting patiently to be filled with his Spirit? Are we ready to focus our minds on Jesus, while uttering his holy name in our hearts so that the world will grow strangely dim?

17 Professionalizing Youth Ministry

Sociologist Max Weber delineated the process by which a vital movement becomes an efficient but lifeless bureaucracy. He called this process "the increasing tendency toward rationalization."[1] The most noticeable evidence of this transition can be found in the replacement of what he calls "charismatic leadership" with "rational leadership."

In his book *Social and Economic Organization,* Weber describes how charismatic leaders initiate movements and enable them to grow in size and significance. He goes on to demonstrate how such movements, because they are successful, must become organized along rational bureaucratic lines. This transformation of a dynamic movement into a rationally prescribed program necessitates the replacement of the spontaneous, untrained charismatic leader with a professionally trained organizer who has the skills essential for this new system.

GIFT VS. TECHNIQUE

The charismatic leader gains influence and effectiveness because he or she possesses special gifts. People are drawn to the charismatic leader's dynamic personality. Charismatic leaders inspire movements filled with euphoria and excitement. Their followers are confident that they are the vanguard of a new era that will transform the world. They're convinced that they are the "new wine in the old wineskins." They're positive that they are part of a divine mission and that history will be altered because of what they do.

In contrast to the charismatic leader (who has no special training for his or her role), the rational leader is professionally trained. This latter type, according to Weber, relies on technique rather than dynamism to get things done. These techniques, designed to maximize efficiency in reaching the prescribed goal, have been established through scientific means. Observation, testing, and evaluation of the best way to accomplish the desired ends motivate the rational leader to adopt "proven" methodology.

Rational leaders are organizers and planners, working to establish a program that will unfold with predictability and order. Hence, they are opposed to the charismatic leader who, like the wind, "blows wherever it pleases. You hear its sound, but you cannot tell where it comes from or where it is going" (John 3:8a).

A BRIEF HISTORY OF YOUTH MINISTRY

A careful sociological analysis of the history of youth ministry reveals that Weber's expectations are being realized. Christian youth work, virtually unknown a century ago, emerged under the charismatic leadership of the almost-forgotten *Christian Endeavor* movement. This interdenominational ministry spread like wildfire to churches not only across America but also around the world. It was led by young people and guided by lay advisors. It inspired countless numbers of young people to Christian vocations and infused churches with evangelistic fervor. Its very success was its downfall.

Bureaucratic denominational leaders sensed that this ecumenical movement was obliterating the importance of denominational distinctives in the minds of their young people. Consequently, many denominations established a youth department with seminary graduates (rational leaders) in charge. The Westminster Fellowship, the Baptist Youth Fellowship, the Luther League, the Methodist Youth Fellowship, and a host of other denominational organizations directed by "experts" in the field of youth work displaced the lay-led youth ministries that marked the early part of the twentieth century. The professionals began taking charge, and the unpaid, untrained charismatic leaders had had their day.

But following World War II, church leaders became aware that young people were again not being reached and challenged effectively. The social and moral shock waves that the war had set off throughout America had left many young people in a state of social and religious rootlessness.

The rationally structured denominational programs seemed devoid of the excitement and creativity essential for those spiritually perilous days. As Weber points out, rational leaders are too conditioned by research conducted in the past to respond instinctively to the requisites of the present and the future. The needs of the times created what Weber called "an elective affinity" for a new movement, and responding to that need was *Youth for Christ.*

The Youth for Christ rallies of the late 1940s and '50s are often looked on with condescending smiles by contemporary youth workers. But we must remember that these rallies were intensely relevant and meaningful to a generation of young people.

The movement spread everywhere. Nearly every city or town had its Saturday-night Youth for Christ rally. Lives were changed, missionaries were recruited, marital matches were made, and a good time was had by all. However, in time the leadership of Youth for Christ became increasingly professionalized, and like all professionals, they became riveted to the "proven" techniques they had always used. They held on to the rallies a bit too long; this created the "elective affinity" for a new movement called *Young Life.*

Whereas Youth for Christ tried to reach young people through rallies held in public halls, Young Life tried to evangelize and disciple young people through club meetings held in private homes. This style of ministry proved to be just

195

what was needed, and its success was soon imitated by Youth for Christ as they (for the most part) abandoned the rally format and opted for the club approach by establishing the *Campus Life* program.

Once again the rational leaders of bureaucratic denominations became concerned. Young Life, Campus Life, and their imitators (such as the *Student Venture* groups of Campus Crusade) seemed to be detached from the institutional church. The promoters of the parachurch organizations contended they were winning young people *for* the church, but the fact remained that a lot of young people got lost on the road from the clubs to the churches. Church leaders became increasingly aware of the need for youth workers who could do in local churches what Young Life and Campus Life were doing in their clubs.

It didn't take much insight to recognize that Bible colleges and seminaries (the source of rational leaders for the Christian church) lacked the skills or understanding required to train contemporary youth workers. And when they looked for resources to train youth workers to program youth groups in local churches, none seemed to be available.

Then, around 1970, two disaffected Youth for Christ leaders, Mike Yaconelli and Wayne Rice, began Youth Specialties. They compiled resources for church youth groups (*Ideas* books) and initiated the National Youth Workers Convention. The Youth Specialties team soon added one-day training seminars, books about youth work, and an assortment of other resources. In 1984, Youth Specialties launched *Youthworker,* a professional journal for youth ministers.

Little did this team recognize the role they were playing in professionalizing modern youth workers. They didn't plan to (in the words of Weber) "routinize charismatic leadership" and make youth work into a set of techniques; but then, results don't always parallel intentions. Since the early '70s, other groups like Youth Specialties have emerged (the

Group organization, for example), and suddenly we have on our hands a rational profession, complete with its own mystique.

Like all rationalized professionals, the Youth Specialties team has looked for guidance from social-science experts rather than encouraging uninformed spontaneity. The National Youth Workers Convention has increasingly used prominent psychologists and sociologists to create the ideological basis of youth work—people like psychiatrist M. Scott Peck and child psychologist David Elkind. Seminars that explain the relevance of Jean Piaget, Erik Erikson, and Lawrence Kohlberg to youth work highlight the convention's agenda. Even the music is performed by professional singing groups, who in their own way have reduced the music ministry into rationalized form.

HARD QUESTIONS

These comments are meant not as negative judgment, but as sociological observation. After all, I too am one more social scientist contributing to the "increasing tendency toward rationalization." However, we need to raise some hard questions about this process. And we need not only to ask the questions but also to face the value judgments that will inevitably follow the answers we get.

First, *does Christianity somehow betray its essential nature when a ministry engages in the "routinization of charisma" and the establishment of professional leadership?* Wasn't the early church so successful in penetrating the Greco-Roman world *because* it was devoid of professionalism? Tentmakers, bakers, and oil-lamp makers were the ministers who spread the gospel. In 1 Corinthians we read:

> For it is written, "I will destroy the wisdom of the wise, and the cleverness of the clever I will thwart." Where is the wise man? Where is the scribe? Where is the debater of this age? Has not God made foolish the wisdom of the world? For since, in the wisdom of God, the world did

not know God through wisdom, it pleased God through the folly of what we preach to save those who believe.

For consider your call, brethren; not many of you were wise according to worldly standards, not many were powerful, not many were of noble birth; but God chose what is foolish in the world to shame the wise, God chose what is weak in the world to shame the strong, God chose what is low and despised in the world, even things that are not, to bring to nothing things that are (1 Cor. 1:19–20, 26–28 RSV).

Don't these verses suggest that the wisdom of "this world" is of little worth when it comes to communicating the gospel? Before we say "Yes, but . . . ," let's admit that many fundamentalist or Pentecostal churches have youth programs directed by charismatic leaders with little or no professional training, and yet these programs impact young people's lives in ways that defy rational explanation.

The size of these lay-led youth groups staggers our imaginations and often forces us to make the bogus claim that the size of a youth group is of no importance. Let's be honest enough at least to consider the possibility that those nonprofessionals have something that we specially trained workers have lost. Let's at least entertain the possibility that there's something about a vital Christian movement that abhors professionalism.

Second, *do we professionals in youth ministry know as much as our employers think we know*—or for that matter, as much as *we* think we know? We learn the professional jargon and use code phrases like "relational theology" and "earn the right to be heard"—phrases that make us special in the eyes of awed amateurs. But is what we say substantially different from what is common knowledge to all mature Christians? Questions like these are going to be asked of us, not only by suspicious church treasurers, but also by some of the most prominent members of the academic community.

Sociologist Christopher Lasch contends that most of

those who have degrees in psychology and sociology think they know more than they really do. He asks whether those who write books on adolescent psychology really understand the minds and motivations of teenagers or whether they are simply clothing their guesses in professional terminology. He wonders whether sociological professionals who work with troubled youth really know how to help their clients, or whether they are simply highly paid degree holders who frantically grasp at fads in therapy in the hope of finding something that may work. Lasch would ask us, who are youth workers, if we deserve the trust that people place in us.[2]

Third, *are professionals, including youth ministry professionals, to a greater or lesser degree con artists?* In his classic book *The Presentation of Self in Everyday Life,* Erving Goffman, a brilliant sociological theorist, argues that we create extensive educational programs for professional roles not because there's so much to learn but because the programs enhance the status of the professional and make him or her seem deserving of a high salary. "Does it *really* take ten years to train a doctor, six years to train a lawyer or seven years to train a member of the clergy," he asks, "or are these years in higher education part of the con job?"[3]

The public is led to believe that professionals spend all of that time in the universities because there's so much to learn in their respective fields. Little do the common folk know that most of the courses taken during those long years of training are either totally unrelated to the professional's field or of such little consequence that those who take them have little memory of their content.

Goffman goes on to claim that the reason the professional's con jobs are so effective is that those who are being conned want to be conned, thereby contributing further to the mystique of competency that professionals try so hard to project. This certainly is true for some of us in youth work. The members of our local churches *want* to believe that youth work is too complicated and difficult for non-professional volunteers to do. The people in the pews *want* to be convinced that they're failing in their Christian responsibility to the young people of their church if they don't hire someone who *really* understands young people.

Most church members are confused by the youth culture; they don't understand the folkways and mores of the high-school social system; and they're threatened by, if not afraid of, adolescents. Consequently, church members find comfort in believing that there is a group of professionally trained youth workers who really understands what's going on with young people and who knows how to handle them. Hiring one of these experts to look after their young people relieves them of the responsibility of participating in the spiritual growth and nurture of the young people in their church.

The mystique of professionalism that we project justifies their desire to turn their young people over to us. The mystique of professionalism gives us justification for making youth work a full-time vocation. But do we *really* know more than parents do about their own young people? Isn't it a bit arrogant to claim that we understand their children—whom they've raised from birth—better than they do? Could it be possible that we are con artists who have bought our own con jobs because the people in our churches have come to believe in us?

I know it must seem strange to use the works of social-science professionals to question the validity of professionalism. But that, I contend, is the role of honest professionals. If we are committed to the preservation of that "charisma," the spontaneous essence that is so essential to any authentically Christian ministry, we must not turn away from the hard questions and their equally hard answers, no matter how discomforting they may be. And besides, who else has the audacity to ask such questions, if we don't?

Conclusion:
The State of Youth
Ministry

The state of youth ministry is, for the most part, a middle-class phenomenon. This comes as no surprise, since only relatively affluent churches have the money to hire youth workers and run first-class youth programs. Youth workers are seldom found among the urban poor in Chicago or with the socially disinherited in Appalachia, even though young people in such places are usually more open to Christian outreach programs than are the WASPs in suburbia.

AN EROSION OF CHRISTIAN VALUES

The suburban captivity of youth work can be discerned first of all in the value formation and ideology of contemporary youth ministry. In an effort to be relevant, youth leaders gradually have allowed an erosion of the values and standards we hold up as guidelines for Christian life and practice. Even though we have an arsenal of talks and Bible studies that exhort our young people to stand up for Christ and be different from the world, we ourselves are seldom ready to disagree with our kids about ethical and cultural issues. We are terrified they might reject us.

EMBRACING ROCK MUSIC

This acquiescence to dominant cultural strains is most evident in the area of rock music. Rock music is not simply an expression of a consciousness; it's a *generator* of a consciousness. Anyone who stands back and looks at our culture objectively will recognize that current rock music is not simply an artistic expression; it's an instrument of rebellion. And it's frightening to realize that the values expressed through much of rock music are antithetical to the values prescribed by the Bible.

Sadly enough, instead of standing against the defiance and deviance advocated by the rock subculture, many of us in youth ministry have tried to go along with the tastes of our kids and have adjusted to rock music and the lifestyle it suggests, hoping thus to keep our rock-loving teenagers within the fold of the Christian youth group. What we fail to realize is that as we accept rock music's expressions of rebellion as normal, we only force young people to seek more extreme ways to express their rebellion.

Radical sociologist Herbert Marcuse of San Diego State University foresaw this process in his book *One Dimensional Man*.[1] Marcuse recognized the tendency of those who control the consciousness of society to co-opt gradually all expressions of rebellion, making a revolutionary consciousness impossible. Rebellion, according to Marcuse, is a necessary stage through which all teenagers must go. But our culture has robbed teenagers of the means to express their rebellion by absorbing expressions of opposition into the culture as legitimate forms of entertainment.[2]

One particularly seductive way that Christian youth workers have tried to co-opt the instruments of rebellion and make them into instruments of evangelism is in our propagation of Christian rock music. The thinking runs, "If rock is the medium that communicates with young people, it only makes sense to give them the gospel through rock." Consequently, youth workers all too uncritically accept the whole array of Christian rock musicians who inundate Christian youth gatherings.

Nevertheless, this receptivity to rock music as a viable medium for communicating the gospel ignores what every expert in communication since Marshall McLuhan has assumed: "The medium is the message." The lyrics are not the most important part of the song, according to the experts.

What is important is the total *gestalt* of the music, the unspoken lifestyle that it connotes and the value system that it represents: dress styles, mores, attitudes, modes of sexual behavior, orientations to the dominant culture, dispositions to family life, and states of religious consciousness. When young people become absorbed in a particular brand of music, they simultaneously tend to adopt the subcultural system that style of music evokes.

Obviously, then, those of us working with youth groups should be evaluating whether or not the *gestalt* generated by rock music is Christian or anti-Christian. We must be sensitive to the sociological ramifications of the several types of Christian rock—soft, hard, punk, or whatever—and should seek to discern how those ramifications relate to the requisites of biblically prescribed discipleship. I'm not suggesting that we reject all rock music. I'm suggesting that we should honestly critique the cultural ramifications of all forms of contemporary Christian music from a Christian perspective. This evaluation should include such factors as the tendency toward materialism by many Christian musicians (who often charge huge fees) and the nurturing of near-cultic worship among their fans.

CHRISTIAN NARCISSISM

The most tragic evidence of the capitulation of Christian youth workers to the demands of the WASP, middle-class society is our willingness to cater to the intense narcissism of its children. Middle-class American teenagers are definitely part of the "me generation"; their neurotic self-interest has led many social scientists to believe they may constitute the most egotistical generation in the history of Western culture.[3] Research on contemporary high-school students reveals that they have few, if any, concerns beyond their own immediate world.

Careful analysis reveals that even young people's seemingly altruistic activities are carried out more to feel good or to attract attention to how wonderful they are than from a deep concern for the needs of others. Consequently, it's easier to get kids to donate money for the starving people of Africa while on the high of viewing a Live Aid concert than to get them to do something about the poverty in their own neighborhoods. In many cases, they'll enter into campaigns to help others only if it's fun or makes them look good.

Too often, those of us involved in youth work support such narcissistic inclinations and are more concerned about helping young people be personally fulfilled than helping them to lose themselves in Christian service for the benefit of others. Even when we do motivate young people to be concerned with social issues, we tend to approach such projects with the hope of promoting the self-actualization of our young people.

SEXUAL CONFUSION

Concession by youth workers to the bourgeois, narcissistic value system is also evident in our reluctance to speak out clearly for biblically prescribed sexual norms. During a recent talk I delivered at a large youth convention, I was amazed at the young people's reaction to my declaration that sexual intercourse outside of marriage was condemned by Scripture.[4] Several told me they were offended by my narrow-mindness. One entire youth group confronted me to say they felt that premarital sexual relations in no way hindered their spiritual growth or diminished their Christian commitment. When I asked what their youth minister had to say about this, they informed me that he was neutral on the issue and wasn't about to impose his personal views on them.

Following this discussion, I hunted down their youth minister and asked him whether he was aware of his youth group's opinion about premarital sex. He responded by suggesting that within the context of his theology, sexuality was meant for the self-actualization of the participants and that as long as there was no exploitation involved, he found it hard to be negative about premarital sex.

The self-centeredness of such a perspective on sexual matters is all too obvious. The impact that such activity will have on the lives of these youth—and their parents—is not considered. The societal consequences of premarital sex are ignored. The affront of such sin to the holiness of God is not part of this new "relevant theological framework." All that seems to matter is that the participants find personal fulfillment in their sexual activities.

William M. Kephart, a foremost American authority in the field of family studies, is dismayed that the church often doesn't offer negative absolutes for premarital coitus.[5] He asks whether the future will hold any restrictions on premarital sexual activity if those in the church have nothing to say on the subject. Many social scientists argue that its increasing laxness about teenage sexual mores may represent one of the church's most significant failures in our modern age.

While few of us would openly approve of premarital coitus, many of us condone a relaxing of norms on such practices as petting and fondling. The most recent Yankelovich studies on teenage sexual patterns indicate that even religious young people find little wrong with mutual manipulation of the genitalia to orgasm.[6] Some of us teach, by implication and suggestion, that young people should consider the consequences of what they do sexually; but many of us display an increasing hesitance to call premarital intercourse sin. We are so anxious to prevent any kind of alienation from the youth subculture that we are willing to compromise on biblical prescriptions for sexual behavior.

UNEQUALLY YOKED IS OKAY

In leading youth conferences, I'm intrigued that Christian young people are seldom aware of the necessity of considering only fellow Christians as possible mates. The idea that Christians should not be "yoked together with unbelievers" (2 Corinthians 6:14) is, in most instances, a new idea to them. When I state that Christians must not enter into exogamous marriages, they suggest that I'm introducing something new and nonessential to the Christian lifestyle.

Their reaction leads me to believe that, for the most part, youth leaders in churches don't deal with this issue. Yet this may be one of the most dangerous oversights in contemporary youth ministry because, in the long run, the selection of a marital partner is often the most decisive factor in the long-term spiritual development of our youth-group members. Once again, the fear of losing our relevant image is the primary source for our reluctance to deal with this essential but disturbing issue.

OPPOSING A DECADENT CULTURAL SYSTEM

Christianity doesn't promise the fulfillment of the American dream. Unfortunately, many youth workers don't seem to be aware of that. We're hired to socialize young people into the dominant values of our middle-class society, and we're usually all too ready to carry out this obligation— even if it means watering down biblical messages that don't readily fit into the value system of typical American teenagers. Our employers, either overtly or subtly, make it clear to us that our job is to keep young people in the church at all costs, including the cost of accommodation to the cultural system in ways that horribly distort the Christian ethic.

True Christianity in our age requires that young people embrace a lifestyle that will set them in opposition to the accepted patterns of the American, middle-class social system. If we youth workers are to do our job properly, we'll have to equip young people to stand against the value orientations and goals prescribed by the dominant community. Not many of us are ready to do that. Most of us believe—or wish—that young people can be followers of Jesus without sacrificing the pleasures and payoffs that come from conformity to the generally accepted cultural standards.

This compromise must end. It's time for youth workers to call young people to the kind of radical Christian commitment that often results in rejection by the world and the loss of success symbols usually delivered to those who accept the yuppie lifestyle.

America is not Christendom. Cultural religion is a subtle imitation of Christianity. It's not the real thing. It's time for us to challenge young people and ourselves to adopt a lifestyle that manifests the difference. If in the process we lose our middle-class audience, we shouldn't fear. The poor and the socially disinherited still wait to hear from us, and they'll hear us just as gladly as they listened to our Master two thousand years ago.

ONE YOUNG BILLION

This past summer the missionary organization I'm involved in, the Evangelical Association for the Promotion of Education, made a concerted effort to reach some of the tens of thousands of teenagers and children who live in the low-cost, government-sponsored housing developments of Philadelphia. We recruited college students who were willing to work without pay. We provided only room, board, and the opportunity to work with some of the most neglected teenagers in America.

Ninety students from twenty-seven colleges volunteered. They discovered the joys that come from working with poor, urban young people. Our volunteers found, for example, that such socially disinherited young people aren't saturated with the recreational alternatives that pervade suburban communities. Youth clubs (patterned after classic Young Life and Campus Life models) drew enthusiastic support. Sports programs reaped broad participation. Outdoor evangelistic meetings were welcomed.

By the end of the summer, many of our college volunteers were convinced that young people living in the poor communities of our city represented one of the most receptive (albeit unreached) "hidden people" in the world.[7] Several collegians, as a direct result of their summer experiences, are prayerfully considering how they can become urban missionaries. They claim that the openness of inner-city young people has spoiled them and made it difficult to consider going back to minister among suburban young people who, by comparison, seem indifferent to the gospel.

If these college volunteers do follow their inclinations to be missionaries among inner-city young people, they'll find that little groundwork has been done for them. We have no *Ideas* books designed for the distinctive cultural orientations of urban young people. No seminars or seminary courses, to my knowledge, equip workers to understand how to handle the peculiar and horrendous problems young people face on city streets. Little if any money is available from churches to carry on this kind of youth work. Missionaries who choose to work with the urban poor will find that they are, for the most part, on their own. Those who work in the worn-out cities of America must learn to invent programs and styles of ministries as they go.

This tragic oversight of such a potentially fruitful mission field isn't confined to the United States. Youth work is seldom considered as a distinct ministry on the foreign fields. We send missionaries who are experts in agronomy, education, and medical science, but we've done almost nothing to train and send cross-cultural youth workers. Anyone who has visited mission fields will immediately recognize what an immense failure this has been. Children and teenagers in Third World countries (now frequently called the *two-thirds* nations because they contain two-thirds of the world's population) are extremely receptive to any gestures of concern or interest directed to them. A student of mine once walked through a small village in the mountains of the Dominican Republic, carrying a volleyball in his hand. He waved the young people of the village to follow him and signaled to them that he wanted to play a game. By the time that Pied Piper got to the edge of the village, he had every teenager with him. The village young people played with him and visited together, and then he shared the gospel with them.

Stories like this ought to be repeated around the world. Unfortunately, they're not—because in most of the two-thirds nations, youth work is almost completely ignored by missionary organizations. Orphanages are started for children and economic development programs are initiated for adults, but little is designed for the adolescents of the two-thirds nations. Ironically, we've ignored youth ministry as a form of foreign missions, even though 90 percent of the population in the two-thirds nations are under the age of twenty-five and more than 30 percent of the population are teenagers. The Marxists have not ignored this fact; in every two-thirds nation I've visited, Marxists have organized a vital youth program.

AT STAKE: THE WORLD

The future of civilization, then, may well be determined by the extent to which the Christian church makes youth ministry to the American urban and two-thirds nations' poor a priority of its missionary program. The time has come for organizations like Youth Specialties, Group, and denominational youth departments to make a concentrated effort to provide training and resources for those who would go to these unreached, hidden peoples of the world. The time has come for us to escape from our suburban, WASP ghettos and discover the excitement and opportunity awaiting us on the mission fields of urban America and the two-thirds nations. The people there may in fact be the only ones left receptive to the transforming message of Jesus Christ; and if we ignore them, others are waiting to reap their allegiance.

Notes

CHAPTER 1

1. See, Will Herberg, *Protestant-Catholic-Jew* (New York: Anchor Books, 1960).
2. See, Edgar Z. Friedenberg, *Coming of Age in America* (New York: Vintage Books, 1963).
3. Robert N. Bellah, Richard Madsen, William M. Sullivan, Ann Swidler, and Steven M. Tipton, *Habits of the Heart* (Berkeley: University of California Press, 1985).
4. Richard Bach, *Jonathan Livingston Seagull* (New York: Macmillan Press, 1970).
5. Ernest Becker, *The Denial of Death* (New York: The Free Press), pp. 15–20, 30–34.
6. *Ibid.* In this book Becker makes heroism the ultimate form of therapy against the anxieties of teenagers.

CHAPTER 2

1. Emile Durkheim, *The Rules of Sociological Method* (Chicago: The University of Chicago Press, 1938, p. 13). Defines a social fact as "ways of acting, fixed or not, capable of exercising on the individual an external constraint; or again, every way of acting which is general throughout a given society, while at the same time existing in its own right independent of its individual manifestations."
2. See, Edward C. Banfield, *The Unheavenly City Revisited* (New York: Little, Brown and Company, 1968), pp. 52–77.
3. WASP is a term used to refer to White Anglo-Saxon Protestants. It was coined by E. Digby Baltzell. See *The Protestant Establishment* (New York: Vintage Books, 1966).
4. "Pure type" is a term employed by Max Weber. See, Max Weber, *Basic Concepts in Sociology*, translated by H. P. Secher (New York: The Citadel Press, 1964, pp. 51–55). A "pure type" is a hypothetical construct which is created out of what are theorized to be the essential characteristics of a phenomenon, which can be used to compare and measure actual phenomena.
5. Gwen Linkead, "On a Fast Track to the Good Life," *Fortune Magazine*, 101(7) (April 7, 1988): 74–78.

6. See, Max Weber, *The Protestant Ethic and the Spirit of Capitalism*, translated by Talcott Parsons (New York: Charles Scribner's Sons, 1958).
7. At Eastern College in St. Davids, Penn., a graduate program has been established to train "entrepreneurs for biblical justice."
8. This imagery taken from 1 Corinthians 13 will be used often in the course of this book.

CHAPTER 3
1. Charles H. Cooley, *Human Nature and the Social Order* (New York: Schocken, 1909), pp. 182–185.
2. Peter L. Berger and Thomas Luckmann, *The Social Construction of Reality* (Garden City, New York: Anchor Books, 1967), Chapter III.
3. See, M. Scott Peck, *The Different Drum: Community Making & Peace* (New York: Simon and Schuster, 1987). This book gives a good survey of the spiritual and psychological dimensions of community.
4. Herman Schmalenbach, "The Sociological Category of Communion" in *Theories of Society*, ed. Talcott Parsons (New York: The Free Press, 1965), p. 331.
5. Irving Goffman, *The Presentation of Self in Everyday Life* (Garden City: Doubleday Anchor Books, 1959), pp. 43–44.
6. See, R. P. Cuzzort, *Humanity and Modern Sociological Thought* (New York: Holt, Rinehart and Winston, Inc., 1969), p. 175.

CHAPTER 4
1. David Riesman with Nathan Glazer and Reven Denney, *The Lonely Crowd* (New Haven, Connecticut: Yale University Press 1961), pp. 17–20.
2. *Ibid.*, pp. 70–81.
3. Erik Erikson, *Identity: Youth and Crisis* (New York: W. W. Norton and Company, Inc.), p. 212ff.
4. Neil Postman, *The Disappearance of Childhood* (New York: Dell Publishing Co., 1982), p. 81ff.
5. Gibson Winter, *Love and Conflict* (Garden City: Dolphin Books, 1958), Chapter VIII.

CHAPTER 5
1. A good summary of the Kinsey studies can be found in Robert R. Bell, *Premarital Sex in a Changing Society* (Englewood, New Jersey: Prentice-Hall, Inc., 1966), Chapter IV.

2. *Ibid.*
3. Ira Reiss and Frank Furstenberg, "Sociology and Human Sexuality," in Harold Lief and Arno Karlen, eds., *Sexual Health Care* (Chicago: American Medical Association, 1980), p. 6.
4. David Elkind, *All Grown Up and No Place to Go* (Reading: Massachusetts, Addison-Wesley Publishing Co., Inc., 1984), pp. 45–60.
5. Bell, pp. 94–96.
6. Ira L. Reiss, *The Social Context of Premarital Sexual Permissiveness* (New York: Holt, Rinehart and Winston, Inc., 1967), Chapter VII.
7. See, Martin Buber, *I and Thou*, translated by Walter Kaufmann (New York: Charles Scribner's Sons, 1970).

CHAPTER 6
1. H. Richard Niebuhr, *The Social Sources of Denominationalism* (New York: The World Publishing Company, 1957), pp. 21–25.
2. Peter Berger, *The Noise of Solemn Assemblies* (Garden City: Doubleday, 1960). In this book Berger uses the concept of "the o.k. world" to connote the attitude of acceptance of the society as basically good.
3. Will Herberg, *Protestant-Catholic-Jew* (Garden City: Anchor Books), Chapter III.
4. Luther P. Gerlach and Virginia H. Hine, *People, Power and Change* (Indianapolis: Bobbs-Merrill, 1970), p. 125.

CHAPTER 7
1. Calvin S. Hall, *A Primer of Freudian Psychology* (New York: The New American Library, 1955).
2. William M. Kephart and Davor Jedlicka, *The Family Society and the Individual*, 6th edition (New York: Harper and Row, 1988), pp. 271–274.
3. Lewis A. Coser, *Masters of Sociological Thought*, 2nd ed. (New York: Harcourt, Brace & Jovanovich, 1977), pp. 220–47.
4. Charles Horton Cooley, *Sociological Theory and Social Research* (New York: Holt, Rinehart & Winston, 1930), pp. 290ff.
5. Bernie Zilbergeld, *The Shrinking of America* (Boston: Little, Brown and Co., 1983).
6. Christopher Lasch, *Haven in a Heartless World* (New York: Basic Books, 1975), chapter 5.

7. Anthony J. Sutch and Miles A. Vich, *Reading in Humanistic Psychology* (New York: Free Press, 1969).
8. Anthony Campolo, *Partly Right* (Waco, Texas: Word Books, 1985).
9. William Glasser, *Stations of the Mind* (New York: Harper & Row, 1981).
10. Jay E. Adams, *Competent to Counsel* (Nutley, New Jersey: Presbyterian and Reformed, 1970).

CHAPTER 8
1. Blaise Pascal, *Penseés* (New York: E. P. Dutton and Co., 1908), Section IV, Fr. 194.
2. An excellent review of the life and thought of Pascal can be found in Emile Cailliet, *Pascal: The Emergence of Genius* (New York: Harper and Row, 1961).
3. For a thorough survey of how the Abraham story plays itself out in the writings of Søren Kierkegaard, see "Abraham and Hegel" in Robert L. Perkins, ed., *Kierkegaard: Fear and Trembling: Critical Appraisal*, Tuscaloosa: University of Alabama Press, 1983).
4. Robert K. Merton, *On Theoretical Sociology* (New York, The Free Press, 1967), pp. 157–171.

CHAPTER 9
1. For an easy-to-understand description of Erik Erikson's theory of stages see Alex Thio, *Sociology: An Introduction* (3rd Edition) (New York: Harper and Row, 1986), pp. 136–138.
2. David Reisman with Nathan Glazer and Revel Denny, *The Lonely Crowd* (New Haven, Connecticut: Yale University Press, 1961) p. 48ff.
3. Ernest Becker, *The Denial of Death* (New York, The Free Press, 1973), pp. 15–20; 30–34.
4. Peter L. Berger and Thomas Luckmann, *The Social Construction of Reality* (Garden City: Anchor Books, 1967), p. 147ff.

CHAPTER 10
1. A good review of trends in illegitimate births can be found in Charles Murray, *Losing Ground* (New York: Basic Books, Inc., 1984), pp. 125–129.
2. Phillippe Aries, *Centuries of Childhood*, translated by Robert Baldick (New York: Alfred A. Knopf, 1984), p. 103ff.

3. Betty Friedan, *The Second Stage* (New York: Summit Books, 1981).

4. See Chapter II in my book, *20 Hot Potatoes Christians Are Afraid to Touch* (Dallas: Word Publishing, 1988), for an elaboration of this controversial claim.

CHAPTER 11

1. See, W. S. F. Pickering, *Durkheim on Religion* (Boston: Routledge and Kegan Paul, 1975), pp. 129–139; 245–248. Emile Durkheim, *The Elementary Forms of Religious Life*, trans. Joseph W. Swain (New York: The Free Press, 1965), Book 2, Chapter 7, Parts II and IV.

2. William James, *Varieties of Religious Experiences* (New York: The New American Library, 1958), pp. 76–139.

3. Carl G. Jung, *The Psychology of the Unconscious* (New York: Dodd, Mead, 1928) p. 199.

CHAPTER 12

1. Søren Kierkegaard, *The Present Age* trans. by Alexander Dru (New York: Harper and Row, 1962), p. 33.

2. Herbert Marcuse, *One-Dimensional Man* (New York: Beacon Press, 1961), pp. 56–83.

3. See, Vance Packard, *The Sexual Wilderness* (New York: David McKay Company, Inc., 1968).

4. *Op. cit.*, Marcuse, see Chapter III.

5. George Herbert Mead, *Mind, Self and Society* (Chicago: University of Chicago Press, 1934), p. 100ff.

CHAPTER 13

1. See, Eric Hoffer, *The True Believer* (New York: Harper and Row, Inc., 1951).

2. See, Lewis A. Coser, *Masters of Sociological Thought*, 2nd edition (New York: Harcourt Brace Jovanovich, Inc., 1977), p. 223ff.

3. See, W. F. Ogburn and M. F. Nimkoff, *Technology and the Changing Family* (Cambridge: Massachusetts, The Riverside Press, 1955), Chapter I, and Census Bureau (1985).

CHAPTER 14

1. Max Weber, *The Theory of Social and Economic Organization*, trans. by Talcott Parsons (New York: The Free Press, 1964), pp. 363–373.

2. *Ibid.*, pp. 367–373.

3. Ernest Becker, *The Denial of Death.*
4. *The Sociology of Georg Simmel,* ed. and trans. by Kurt H. Wolf (New York: The Free Press, 1959), pp. 87–177. See his seminal essay, "Quantitative Aspects of the Group," given in these pages.

CHAPTER 15
1. Ronald J. Sider, *Rich Christians in an Age of Hunger* (Downers Grove: InterVarsity Press, 1977), Chapter II.
2. Quoted in H. Richard Niebuhr, *The Social Sources of Denominationalism* (New York: The World Publishing Company, 1964), pp. 70–71.

CHAPTER 16
1. Henry Steele Commager, *The American Mind* (New Haven: Yale University Press, 1950), pp. 164–171.

CHAPTER 17
1. See, H. H. Gerth and C. Wright Mills, *From Max Weber* (New York: Oxford University Press, 1964), pp. 51–55.
2. See, Christopher Lasch, *Haven in a Heartless World* (New York: Basic Books, 1977). This entire book gives an excellent review of how professionalization in "helping" sciences has developed.
3. See, Erving Goffman, *The Presentation of Self in Everyday Life* (Garden City: Doubleday Anchor Books, 1959). In this book Goffman provides a careful review of how social roles are contrived and maintained. Some have contended that Goffman has made a study out of studying the phony. See Ray P. Cazzort and Edith King, *20th Century Social Thought,* 3rd Edition (New York: Holt, Rinehart and Winston, Inc., 1980), pp. 286–293.

CONCLUSION
1. Herbert Marcuse, *One Dimensional Man* (Boston: Beacon Press, 1966).
2. Bill Gaither, the famous gospel musician, contends that modern music has become one of the most divisive influences in our modern world. He insists that different forms of music create different subcultures. He contends music is the major cause of social gaps between parents and children.

3. Christopher Lasch, *The Culture of Narcissism* (New York: Norton, 1978), chapter 1.
4. See 1 Thessalonians, 4:3–7.
5. William M. Kephart, *The Family, Society and the Individual*, 5th ed. (Boston: Houghton Mifflin Company, 1981), pp. 281ff.
6. Daniel Yankelovich, *New Rules: Searching for Self-Fulfillment in a World Turned Upside Down* (New York: Bantam, 1981).
7. The term *hidden people* was developed by those who have developed the Church Growth movement and refers to those who have been overlooked in the propagation of the gospel.